THE UNFOLDING

A Journey of Involution

J. S. WOLFE

"Life is not a journey of becoming, but one of Unfolding."

— *J.S. WOLFE*

CONTENTS

DEDICATION & GRATITUDE

To my brother, Marco Salem, for your love, support, and protection. To my niece, Nadine Soliman, for the amazing design.
To my dog, Vincent, and my cats, Fluffy and Jojo; You saved my life in more ways than I can count.
To my mother, departed father, both my sisters, and my beautiful extended family, who believed in me and encouraged me to write.
To my friends, Mariam Aly, Khalid Khalil, and Dahlia El Sioufy, you are my loving anchors.
To Karim Elias, for his generous guidance and feedback.
To my angel Farshid Gazor, who always watches over me. Your prayers keep me safe.
To Vincent Vieluf for trusting me with his amazing work.
To my therapist, Dr. Mostafa Shaheen, who kept me sane enough to finish this book, and to my Hypnotherapist Pierre-Etienne Vannier, who initiated the unearthing of my inner light.
To my Ayahuasca family, for the loving presence.
To the Universe, for blessing me with all of you.
Namaste

PRELUDE

We are a mess, and we are here to pull it back
together.

There was a gun in my right hand, a bunch of pills in my left, a
steep hill beneath me, and a stalker right behind me. I wanted to
die thinking the pain will end and bliss will begin. I was sick
with the world and the growing coldness of everyone in it. I
asked for forgiveness for what was left behind and what was to
come. A small puppy interrupted my prayer, knocking over the
pills off my hand. They rolled down the hill. Everything
accelerated and slowed down all at once. I picked up the puppy
with my free hand, and slowly pushed the gun away behind us
to avoid an accident. I held the puppy close to me as I leaned
back then lied down on my back to catch my breath. Someone
picked up the gun. This was the first time my stalker looked
concerned. He had no intention of assaulting me. He needed to
save me. I realized at that moment how he needed me a lot more
than I needed him.

My suicidal ideations didn't end there. I was coming to terms with removing this option off the table. After all, my previous attempts that bordered on success, bought me a few minutes of bliss at best before I was jolted back to life. Clearly, I was meant to stay. A voice told me this is not the way to go at this time.

The universe sent me many saviors throughout my life. My puppy asked me to stay. My two rescue cats demanded it. A psychopath challenged me to love myself. With a pen, a funny bone, a DMT pipe, a plane ticket to the Netherlands, and a refillable Ayahuasca shot glass showed me how to stay. I became receptive to the idea of living, without frantically trying to escape. My desperation to end my pain made me willing to take a deep dive into the dark void of the inner paths, right through the tunnel. The way was only forward through it until I would see some light. I didn't realize I would cower once inside, and that I no longer had a say about changing my mind. I had to keep going until my work was done. The work is always forgiveness. The gateway to forgiveness is empathy, and there is no empathy without a proper understanding of the human heart.

* * *

INTENTION

Nature is in perfect order. It is up to us to align
with its flow. The roadmap is empathy.

There is much to be learned about human behavior through
Drama. The healing path may or may not have shortcuts, yet I
believe in the power of sharing and planting seeds. The
intention of this book is to plant a garden of empathy. If you are
a psychopath, sociopath, narcissist, or anyone low on empathy
reading this, I know you are capable of cold empathy at best,
and you can put it to good use, if you know what's good for you.
I will make some suggestions to reach your goals with the least
amount of damage to yourself and others.

Without empathy, all will be eventually destroyed.
It is the pathway to understanding ourselves
and others. It is our compass towards our
destination. We must make sure it's pointing in
the right direction.

I HAVE BEEN coaching actors and writers for a decade now and chasing psychopaths for the past 20 years. Allowing myself to be coached through whatever life brought into my path is one of my biggest blessings. Learning how to be good students is detrimental to our well-being. I couldn't help but notice how fast self-knowledge can fluctuate. One day you think you know who you are, and another you have no idea what the hell is going on. Change is constant; therefore, surrender to the process is important. I believe change can be embraced when we remain connected to source energy. There is something stable, that is, our core. This is what we need to hold onto as our anchor. Without this anchor, we do fly off the handle. Source energy is the constant that is omnipresent. All else is the variable, be it people, circumstances, locations, thoughts or emotions. We can withstand anything when we identify ourselves with the constant and not the variables.

May you remain well-anchored, so you may travel
safely, within and without.

Over the years, I observed many people become unhinged. There is a rise in judgments and a decrease in our emotional language proficiency. So much of our suffering is caused by a sense of disconnection, even from our own emotions. Humanity has been going through intense challenges and shifts at such a staggering speed that far outruns our collective stamina. We lost the capacity to keep up. We have all been suffering tremendous overwhelm on many levels. Sadly, many of us resort to numbing, which only, needlessly, intensifies the pain. However, with all changes and challenges come opportunities for growth. We get to shed old skin, as well as unfold beliefs, thoughts, and emotions that no longer serve our highest good. I trust most of us have grown tired of our old patterns. This is a great sign for better shifts to come. I am grateful for such dark times because they always carry the promise of light.

Through my specialty in character analysis and embodiment, the world of entertainment collided naturally with psychology and spirituality. The craft of acting and of writing must not be separated from our chosen reality. They require authenticity, empathy and a deep dive into the human psyche. Since we create our own reality, it is no different from creating characters for the screen. We get to tap into our power of creation.

Having the courage to explore our collective and subjective consciousness, we become receptive to lessons and the healing properties of every living being, including animals, and plants. We cannot understand each other through the lens of judgment and persecution. As a race, we can no longer afford it. Any writer or actor will tell you the number one condition to understand and portray a character authentically is by, first, becoming their strongest advocate no matter how much they oppose their personal beliefs and values. The beauty of this process is in how it humbles us and opens our minds to receiving each other well. Instead of judgment, we use discernment. Lack of judgment does not mean we remove accountability. We may judge the behaviour, without defining the person by it. Our judgments are subjective anyhow.

I hope you reach your highest potential. I am honored to share what I know. I can only hope it saves someone out there, and to be a reminder that you are not alone.

> May you replace addictions with connections;
> hostility with empathy and forgiveness;
> indifference with love. While we may not be
> able to fix the world, we can choose to heal
> ourselves. After all, the most valuable gift you
> can offer the world is your own well-being.

CHAPTER 1
THE WORLD OF EMOTION

It is truly incomprehensible how emotionally
illiterate we have become.

Most people try to hide their emotions. For centuries, we have
been encouraged to suppress them. During the rise of the
corporate mindset, a lack of empathy was favored. Needless to
say, it took a fatal toll on our psyches. We were punished for
being too emotional, too happy, too sad, and for connecting
with natural human emotions. We created a deadly habit of
abandoning our natural feelings. Suppressing emotions led to a
demise in emotional language, communication skills, empathy,
our relationships, and our physical health. Being unable to name
our emotions correctly prevents us from releasing them. There
seems to be a rise in narcissism largely due to emotional
bluntness. We lost connection with our intuition, our needs, and
our bodies.

Anything suppressed comes out in a violent way.

THE SADDEST THING IS, those who are still in touch with their emotions are consistently ridiculed and abandoned, so they numb themselves to avoid being shunned. We get shamed for being human. "You're too sensitive". "Be a man". "You are so dramatic". "Stop crying". "Don't be so weak". We have become emotionally abusive, and then blame the abused for reacting. As long as we judge our emotions, we will not learn our lessons, nor will we be able to contain them over time.

> Judgment is the antonym of empathy. It blocks our understanding. We cannot resolve what we do not understand.

Judging our emotions creates an internal war zone. When you fight against nature, nature prevails. Actors know this. Their job is to release their own emotions, so it doesn't betray them and seep into their performance. They must empathize with their characters. They have to begin from a place of non-judgment. Without understanding, actors resort to dramatic gestures to compensate for this lack. Their performance is over the top. It is insulting to their audience, as well as the voiceless people they represent. When it is time to leave a character, an actor has to go through a process of emotional release, and re-integration.

> Our level of understanding others relies on the depth we understand ourselves. When we are judgmental, it indicates how harsh we are on ourselves. Our emotional struggle is reaching a boiling point due to our lack of self-empathy.

Performers are blessed with an opportunity to release the emotions they stored over the years. Anyone can make their way into acting, for example, but not everyone takes advantage of the healing properties it offers. It takes emotional, mental, physical, psychological, and spiritual sacrifice. These are the courageous few, who leave their mark. Their emotional release is an act of purging on our behalf. Watching them, we feel spent, healed, and elevated. The entertainment business is the first to be censored, especially in the Middle East. Putting limitations on emotional expression and creativity defies the purpose of our work. Censorship is a byproduct of the collective toxic shame and a reflection of how we censor ourselves. The more emotionally censored we are, the more we project our issues on each other. Emotional abuse is at an all-time high. People have become masters at using others' emotions against them. We no longer need to rely on physical confrontations alone. Look at the vicious comments on social media and the rise of emotional abuse in our relationships. From public humiliations, character assassinations to mass shootings in schools, and family annihilators, much of humanity is hell-bent on embodying sociopathic personas. Many thought, "If you can't beat them, join them."

Because we reached a breaking point; however, we are called for emergency mass meditations, shamanic healing ceremonies, and for gathering our courage to share our stories. No one is in it alone. It is vital to regain our emotional fluency once again. Empathy has been under assault by a world that rewards emotional anorexia. We are imploding. Wars are now happening within our hearts and minds. We took all that pent up anger into our homes and schools. Crimes against one's family and friends by unsuspecting, seemingly promising, individuals is jolting us into a rude awakening. Evil has no specific face. It is often hidden behind a smile rather than a scar. Unless we reconnect with our empathy, we will continue to suffer as we struggle with self-love and self-acceptance. Prioritizing self-empathy is the way to elevate our lives and relationships. We all deserve a better quality of life. We can no longer afford to be numb and indifferent. We can break this cycle by reacquainting ourselves with our higher truth and by being open to shift our perceptions.

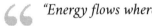 *"Energy flows where attention goes." ~Buddhist Proverb*

MISREPRESENTED EMOTIONAL STATES OF BEING

Some emotions are essential to a healthy state of being. They are necessary abilities that we need to acquire. Some of the most critical emotions have lost meaning over time, which is why we lost our ability to embody them. How can we put something into practice, if we don't know how to define them properly anymore? Keeping true definitions alive, eliminates their natural obscurity. Still, all esoteric knowledge is beyond description and requires a personal experience. So, I am sharing the definitions to the best of my ability.

FORGIVENESS

Forgiveness is the ultimate gateway to well-being.

Forgiveness is releasing yourself from the chains of the past. It does not mean that what was done is ok, nor does it mean letting yourself or someone else off the hook. Forgiveness means that what was done to you will no longer have power over you. It will not dictate your future behavior, or cause negative emotions to occupy a permanent residence within you. It is about releasing bitterness, resentment, regret, and anger. Refusing to forgive someone takes away your power, not theirs. In fact, you lose your power to them. Refusing to forgive yourself depletes your life force. Refusing to forgive a situation makes you its hostage.

WHAT HAPPENS *when you do not forgive?*

> Lack of forgiveness is, not only unhealthy but potentially, fatal.

1. You strengthen the toxic bond between you and the one you cannot forgive. Even when the situation is over, their energy is still there controlling you.

2. YOU DENY yourself the opportunity to grow and become a better version of yourself by remaining stuck in an old story that belongs to your old self.

3. YOU DO NOT TAKE the lessons you need, and risk repeating the event by energetic invitation.

4. YOU DEVELOP physical and mental illness. Lack of forgiveness is the cancer of the mind, body, and soul. When you do not release resentment, anger, blame, guilt, and shame, they manifest themselves in physical form and block blessings from entering your life.

5. I BELIEVE that when we die, all things unforgiven come to deal with us. The more we forgive, while we are here, the easier our transition will be when our time is up. This is not scientific. It is a vision I received during an Ayahuasca journey.

Unprocessed emotions form crystals within our body temple, and darken our pattern. This is why we feel heavy when we don't resolve things and hold it in.

How Forgiveness Feels

The first step to freedom is forgiveness.

You feel lighter in your body, your face illuminates and radiates. You invite more blessings into your life. As you reach your highest potential and fulfill your true calling, abundance flows into your life and gratitude becomes your home emotion. You don't need the other person's participation. Forgiveness is a personal cleansing. Inviting the other person back into your life is your choice; however, cutting them off will not feel hostile.

Love

I used to think I'm in love when I'd lose myself in someone... until I loved someone I found myself in.

Love is often confused with attachment, obsession, and addiction. I don't know if it is a describable state. It transcends emotion. It is a consistent state of appreciation. There is no fear in the space of love. There is perpetual gratitude and serenity. Love is the observer, watching everything, without being taken in. We don't get consumed or possessed. It is grounded, all-knowing, all-encompassing and all trusting. With love, there is no judgment. It is the freedom to let things be; it is a state of allowance and receptivity. It is a blissful radiance. We see things in its entirety and accept all its parts. Love is creativity, faith, and beauty. It is expansive. It transcends time and space. It does not discriminate. It has no expectations; only appreciation. I believe the Universe is made of love. It is not about attachment, attraction, and lust. It can be present in our relationships when we each embody the state of love and are able to connect freely and without fear or ownership.

COURAGE

 "Without courage, we cannot practice any other virtue with consistency. We can't be kind, true, merciful, generous, or honest."~Maya Angelou

Courage has a dignified presence to it. When we are in our heart space, we act with integrity and authenticity. Consistency of virtue is, indeed, the dividing line between courage and cowardice. Dr. Brené Brown pointed out that courage comes from Latin "cor" which means heart. So, courage is acting from your heart space. Interestingly, cowardice is associated with faint-heartedness and spinelessness, which implies a lack of integrity. The spine, when perfectly integrated, keeps the body intact. Without integration, we fall apart. When courage is one of our core values, we will do what is right, no matter how challenging it is. Below is a breakdown of some courageous acts, and some popular behaviors among cowards.

 ✶ ✶ ✶

THE COURAGEOUS
1. They are honest with themselves and others.
2. They confront themselves, and situations when called for.
3. They do right by others and themselves without witnesses.
4. They are mindful.

5. They forgive.

6. They confront their own demons.

7. They are reliable, authentic, and humble.

8. They speak up against injustice even if it doesn't directly affect them.

9. They welcome uncomfortable conversations in the name of resolutions.

10. They prioritize their relationships over upsets.

11. They speak to people directly.

THE COWARDS

1. They are passive-aggressive.

2. They backstab others, gossip and slander.

3. They do not forgive.

4. They avoid confrontation and are evasive.

5. They are deceptive and manipulative.

6. They do not accept accountability.

7. They prey on your vulnerabilities.

8. They are ungrateful, unreliable, and careless with others' well-being.

9. They listen to heresy and act accordingly.

10. They make assumptions.

11. They sabotage others' success and good fortune.

NOTE: Not everyone comes from a place of cowardice whenever they behave in the aforementioned ways. Sometimes, they do not have the capacity, or they are unaware of their actions. It can be a learned behavior. Once they figure it out, they can do better. So, look for what is a consistent pattern in someone.

* * *

VULNERABILITY

> Vulnerability is beautiful and honest, they said. It's
> being strong, some said. I am, a walking open
> wound, my ego said. I am..., my soul said. I'll
> keep you safe, the divine said.

Vulnus in Latin means *wound*. *Vulnerare* is the verb, meaning *to wound*. Vulnerability is the susceptibility to be wounded.

VULNERABILITY TAKES GREAT COURAGE, because it comes from the heart space. It is the most honest we can be, which is why it carries great risk. Dr. Brené Brown is the ultimate researcher of our time on this topic. After listening to Dr. Brown, I was perplexed by the number of people shying away from vulnerability. I spent my life carrying my vulnerabilities on my forehead. It was as though I was flaunting my wounds. When people took advantage of that, as they often did, it did not deter me. I thought I was being kind and courageous. In truth, I was subconsciously looking for connection, not realizing I was inviting psychopaths and narcissists into my life. After a while, it took a serious toll. There is so much heartbreak we can endure before we collapse. I would not recommend being recklessly vulnerable. As Dr. Brown reminded us, "Not everyone has earned the right to hear our story."

What is more important than being vulnerable is understanding how sacred it is. Exposing your wounds to those, who did not earn the trust to see them is an act of self-destruction. Dr. Brown also pointed out that JOY is the most terrifying emotion. This hit close to home. My motto for many years was, "I don't want to have anything to lose." Joy was something to be feared. It was usually followed by a divine balancing act, and attracted potent envy that would knock the best of us off our high horse.

ONE DAY, in a DMT ceremony, I had an incredible vision about vulnerability. While it is true that we can be exposed to danger because of it, there is a level of vulnerability that is incredibly powerful. The message was:

There is nothing noble about wearing your wounds as a badge of honor, but there is in accepting, and healing them. Vulnerability is authentic power only when you become so comfortable with your wounds, they become a lighthouse guiding others, and your acceptance leaves nothing for haters to attack. You stand in your power, wounds and all. You are removing the buttons that others try to push. Your fragility becomes your strength. The stronger your light, the more you expose how insignificant your haters are. This is why they spend their lives trying to dim those powerhouses. They do not want to be exposed so . They do not want you to know the worth and potential they see in you, and are threatened by.

AUTHENTICITY

> The level of our authenticity is marked by our
> level of self-deception.

Definitions: **Authenticity** is the quality of being genuine and the part of us that did not get corrupted by life. **Honesty** is honor, decency, and propriety.

When our constructed personality is aligned with and honors our original nature, we become honest. It is when we do not deviate from our very nature. When we think of someone authentic, we often describe them as being made of a fine fiber.

They are not tarnished. We all deviate sometimes from our authenticity, especially when we get out of our heart space and into our heads.

The mind is a skillful trickster. But if you are authentic for the most part, and are not identifying with the few instances when you stepped out of alignment with yourself, you are still considered authentic. It is our responsibility to keep ourselves in check.

When we think of someone, who is inauthentic, most of us cringe at their hypocrisy, and yet, it is wide-spread. Sometimes it is due to self-deception; other times, it's because they chose to identify with the roles others assigned to them for the sake of fitting in. Our level of dishonesty is directly tied with the level of our self-deception.

THERE ARE many factors that lead to inauthenticity and a lack of integration:

1. Fear of judgment, and not being liked.

2. The need to fit in with others overpowers the need to stay true to yourself.

3. Prolonged use of drugs such as heroin, cocaine, and alcohol, leads to an overestimation of oneself, a lack of presence and connection, and in extreme cases can lead to sociopathic/narcissistic behaviors.

* * *

PRACTICE AUTHENTIC LIVING:

1. Check-in with yourself, and your true calling.

2. Feed the connection you have with yourself, and prioritize that over fitting in. Fitting in is the opposite of belonging, because the former requires you to abandon your unique identity, whereas the latter celebrates it. When you are

inauthentic and succeed at fitting in, you will feel perpetually unhappy and alone. You cannot belong without sharing all of who you are.

3. Invest in your passions, creativity, and life's work.

4. Surround yourself with authentic people.

5. Leave any social circle that tries to fit you into their mold.

INTEGRITY

> Find yourself... Find yourself... Find yourself and
> you will find me...

Integrity is when your mind, body, heart, and soul are in full agreement. The root of many people's lack of fulfillment is when they become torn between listening to one part of themselves while denying the other. Often, what the mind is saying to us is based on past experience, or based on what others are telling us to do, think, and feel. They continue fighting against their own natural flow. We are meant to flow with all of Nature, and it is often known through intuition. The mind is tricky as it often masquerades itself as intuition and true heart desires. When it's wrong, as it often is, we blame the heart for it. Fighting against Nature's flow proves painful and futile. Going with the flow means answering your own natural flow that is naturally aligned with Nature's flow. Don't let people shame you for not going with the flow to get you to break your boundaries for them. When each of us aligns in full integrity in our own right, we will naturally flow together, in Nature's concert.

> I go with my flow, not yours.

GRACE

> Grace is allowing the divine force to move
> through us.

Grace is surrender, faith, elegance, and a gentle flow. When we are receptive to grace, we feel blessed, protected, divinely guided, and inspired to take honorable action. It is being able to lead a dignified life. If you ask someone about the meaning of grace, they may struggle with its definition. It ranges between honor, nobility, elegance, among other wonderful things. But if you ask them what it means to disgrace someone, almost everybody will know exactly what you're talking about. When we are saved in the midst of turmoil, we say it was by the grace of God. We feel graced with someone's presence when they are held in high regard. Here is the trouble; grace is divine and does not discriminate. Everyone is equally worthy. It is inherent. When people set out to disgrace someone, it is beyond my comprehension. What level of arrogance must someone have to take away what is inherently yours? There is a massive difference between holding someone accountable for causing harm and disgracing them. Grace is divine. Only psychopaths and narcissists have a god complex, so amazingly delusional, they set out to assassinate and disgrace others. Yet the level of their delusion blinds them to the fact that no one can take away, what they cannot provide. It is not for us to give or take away grace. In the game of pointing fingers, everyone will have a few pointed at them. We point fingers as though we are righteous, innocent, and absolved. If we were, we wouldn't entertain such practices. Everyone is equally guilty or equally innocent. None of us are fit to be judges and jurors.

* * *

Death

> The beauty of death is that everyone will get to
> face the truth then. We will be released then.
> There will be justice then. There will be
> forgiveness then. There will be love then. Until
> then...

Death is a transition into richer life. Until physical death, we can do our best. I wish we could give each other as much mercy in life as we do once we're gone. Death and love are one and the same. We die in each other, and we die to ourselves. We die in passion and we die in creativity. We die in our ego when we die in things that give us life. The only two truths are love and death, and in that, a magnificent bond is created. Both are bonded by killing our ego. This is why the two things we fear most are love and death. In the face of surrender, we retreat. I believe death is the gateway to authentic love. It is the death of everything that is not who we are. We identified with the masks for too long. We merged with our character and abandoned our spirit. Death is energy like everything else in the universe is energy. Scientifically speaking, energy cannot be created or destroyed, but transformed. So, to die is to go through a transformation. I believe, to make the transition easier, we need to practice dying, as much as we can, while we are here. To die while alive is to keep our shadow selves from consuming our soul.

Death to self: We surrender our ego and identify with our soul in conscious moments of truth. Intentional re-invention of the self by surrendering old habits for better ones.

Death by Love: Those authentic love exchanges with friends, family, loved ones, animals, plants, etc.

Death by life: When life brings us to our knees, and we become humbled without self-pity.

THE POWER OF EMOTIONS

We are as sick as our unprocessed emotions.

There are two root emotions from which all others stem:
LOVE and FEAR.

We are driven by one or the other at a given moment. It is easy to distinguish the root of your emotions when choosing between the two. Some characters are clearly acting from a place of fear, while others are mostly acting from a space of love. We can, of course, swing between both; however, most individuals tend to sway more towards one over the other.

Tracing back someone's root emotion, helps us gain a better understanding of why they act the way they do. You can do the same for yourself. We are complex creatures. Addressing the correct emotion helps us towards a resolution. If we address the wrong one, we fall deeper into conflict.

Some emotions can fluctuate between love and fear such as sadness and anger. When we are sad, it can be an opportunity to care for oneself and holding space for ourselves to grieve and heal. However, when our sadness turns to self-pity, is becomes fear-based. Anger, unchecked, can be fear-ridden with bitterness and feelings of vengeance; whereas, turned into passion and creativity, it becomes sacred anger. Ecstasy can be fear-based when we have become delirious from intense grief, which can also deliver us to awakenings and surrender. Meeting the threshold of emotion can catapult it into the other end of its spectrum.

Not all negative emotions are consistently
negative. They can serve a necessary purpose
when channeled properly.

FEAR

> Acronym: False evidence, appearing real.
> Forget everything and run.
> Face everything and rise.

Fear can often save our lives by prompting us to run from danger, freeze when needed, fight when called for, and fawn when it's the only way to survive. Sometimes fear is a protective signal coming from our intuition. If we feel no fear, we will not be able to foresee disastrous consequences, or we may not be inclined to do what is morally right. Being fearless in a relationship may make us take the other person for granted. We need to care for not losing someone we love. Often, fear can act as a motivation to do better and be better at life. The key is to discern when to dismiss fear and when to transform it for something better. The existence of toxic fear is in the space of anticipation. It is a future emotion. We can truly put ourselves in such a horrifying state over imagined worst-case scenarios. When we feel intimidated by a violent person, the torture is in those moments of anticipation. Once attacked, we focus back on the pain of the present moment. On a positive note, those, who skydive, for example, feel the most fear before they jump. Once they do, adrenalin kicks in, and they feel elated.

Often, we have to reach a threshold before we transition into a new emotion. Take physical pain for example. When someone punches you once, it will obviously hurt. When they punch you a few more times in the same area, the pain continues to increase. But if they keep going for much longer, you become numb to the pain. You feel nothing. A while longer still, and the pain will turn into pleasure. You may begin to seek it out. It becomes an addiction.

· · ·

THERE ARE two reasons for this:

1. It is our body's way of dealing with an unpleasant situation by turning it in our favor. The adrenalin pumps enough to make us numb and then delirious. It becomes a drug. Think of all the adrenalin junkies out there.

2. The deeper the emotional pain, not only do we become more tolerant of physical pain, but we begin to use it as a numbing agent to our emotional pain. Think of those, who self-harm, whether through inflicting actual physical harm on themselves or by using other self-destructive means. A history of abuse creates deep emotional wounds that make us susceptible to trauma bonds, which then become the only anesthetic until proper healing is achieved.

ANGER VS. SACRED ANGER

Anger, unchecked, turns free spirits into slaves.

Anger is a secondary emotion; meaning, it is rooted in fear, grief, and disappointment. To heal anger, we must know the underlying emotion. It can come up when we feel scared of losing someone or something. We may fear not being understood, which, in our primitive mind, can mean losing connection, which threatens our very survival. Many people are living in survival mode. Survival mode causes us to suffer from adrenal fatigue. We get stuck in an anger loop.

Anger has proven useful in several life situations. When we are not angry enough about a current situation, we may stay in it much longer than necessary. The best example of this is being in an abusive relationship. It depletes your life force, and anger requires energy and fuel for you to escape. We have to reach a breaking point to become angry over a situation instead of remaining in the roles of victims and enablers. When a woman is abused by her partner, for example, she has to reach a point of saying, "Enough is enough." The trauma bond finally breaks. In less severe circumstances, we, too, can reach our breaking point to end self-destruction. We want to say enough to addiction, laziness, procrastination, and hopelessness. However, anger in itself can be the drug of choice, because of the certainty it offers. You know you are addicted to anger when you express it through indifference, bitterness, passive-aggression, and bullying. We all get angry and that's ok. What is not ok, is to use it consistently, instead of communicating our needs with clarity like grown-ups. Otherwise, it morphs into the quiet, translucent poison infiltrating our system, scattering our focus, while diminishing our confidence, kindness, love, friendships, and success. It is a malignant virus of the soul. We need to become alchemists, who are able to transform our negative anger into sacred anger.

> What we communicate resolves. What we avoid,
> intensifies.

Sacred anger is when we turn rage into passion. We channel it through creativity. The practice of channeling anger through art or sports can be a true life-saver. But you must do so intentionally. Playing sports mindlessly, or for the wrong reasons, does not have a positive impact, as is the case with some people, obsessed with growing muscles without fortifying themselves from within. It is healthy to allow yourself to express your anger, while being mindful. Expressing emotion is far better than allowing it to get magnified by suppression.

The core of toxic anger is our inherent need to be seen and heard. The worst punishment humans endure is to be ignored. This is why some people choose to become infamous when fame is out of reach. Negative attention becomes better than feeling shunned and unworthy of acknowledgment.

To combat toxic anger, identify its root cause, and what you gain by holding on to it. We cannot examine an effect without examining its cause. Because anger is one of those emotions that offers certainty, and a false sense of power, we find it difficult to let go of it. When someone feels powerless, they use anger as a sense of regaining control. Certainty, power, and control are humanity's weakness, and downfall. Many don't grasp that the nature of life is uncertain, control is rarely had, and power is too inconsistent to rely on. You may be certain that through anger, you will intimidate others into doing what you want. You will be heard and seen. You can no longer be ignored. While that may work temporarily, it will neither fulfill you nor earn you people's loyalty or respect. Being feared is an unfulfilling practice. This is why you never get enough of it. Extracting your power by way of anger is like choosing to become a slave to others. You will always need someone to exert your power on. But when you extract your power from within, you are truly powerful and free. You become a master of yourself regardless of what others do.

PROMPTING *questions to ask yourself to regain authentic power:*

What triggers my anger?

What do I gain from being angry?

What are my emotional buttons that, if pressed, I get angry?

How do I express my anger? Am I passive-aggressive or overtly violent?

Am I afraid to speak my mind, and so I use my silence to communicate?

Do I fear accountability? What does my fear say to me, when I am unable to express my truth calmly?

Do I channel it into creative work?

Are there people that trigger my anger more than others?

Why does this particular person/situation trigger my anger?

What needs are not met when I am in conflict with this person? What do I wish they understood so that I don't feel threatened?

Why am I feeling threatened that I have to put up my anger armor?

What will happen if I am not in control of a situation?

Do I get angry when others voice their expectations and impose their ideas on me? Does it threaten my autonomy?

How do I feel when someone's approval and acceptance of me is conditional? Does it make me feel inadequate?

Was there a time in my life when I had no control over a situation, and as a result, I was harmed?

How can I communicate my boundaries in healthier and more effective ways?

* * *

HOME EMOTIONS

Everyone has an emotion they turn to for comfort.
It is their home.

A home emotion is one that is most consistent in a person. Some of us naturally reset to joy, while some gravitate towards sadness. Identify your home emotion.

Look for how it shows up in your life. If your home emotion is gratitude, it will show even in your darkest hour. Your home emotion can change after a traumatic experience, but the original one is still there, buried underneath the new one. Those, whose home emotion is anger, the quality of their relationships suffer as it creates conflict in all aspects of their life. An angry person is rarely genuinely grateful or forgiving. Anger is a manifestation of a deeper problem. Once you know the home emotion, and how it shows up, you can then be mindful of how you behave and feel situation by situation.

Ask how you can connect with your home emotion if it is positive, and how to change it, if it is negative. We cling to our home emotions because it's our comfort zone. The need for familiarity makes us hold on to things, no matter how destructive they are. The pain we are used to feels safer than a pleasure we are not used to. To find emotional health, we need to develop familiarity with healthy emotions.

> There is something to be gained by our chosen
> emotions, no matter how negative. It is why
> many people are addicted to their pain.

When we hold on to our pain, a certain need is met. It is an opportunity to love and care for ourselves. It is a method of getting attention and a way to avoid responsibility. Whenever we play the victim, we evade being accountable for our actions, and pretend to be powerless to make a change.

Those, who suffer from mental illness or a personality disorder, may swing between two conflicting home emotions. They are divided. Think Dr. Jekyll and Mr. Hyde. When there are two or more sets of identities, each personality will have its home emotion. Ted Bundy was split between a hopeless romantic, sociable persona, and one that was enraged and only silenced by committing murder. The average person can suffer a similar divide on a lesser scale. We do not have to be defined by what happened to us, and the consequent emotional pain that was created because of it. We are free to move out of our current emotional location. Some of our learned behaviors that were once useful become damaging later in life. No matter how many personas are at war within you, you can unify them, by duplication. Reset to a unified home emotion, one persona at a time.

Emotional Buttons

> We all have buttons that, when pressed, send us
> into survival mode.

Those buttons represent old pains that have not yet been accepted, dealt with, healed or processed. Unhealed traumas create such buttons. For example, most children, who were abandoned by their parents, grow to become hyper-sensitive to rejection and develop a fear of abandonment.

Any threat of abandonment, whether it is real or imagined, renders the adult into a child, raging, throwing tantrums, or sinking into an anxiety spiral and depression. If we were to heal our buttons, we, first, need to identify them, then recalling the very first incident that created them.

After that, we have a few choices:

1. We process and heal them, so that there is nothing to push.

2. We accept them, so when they do get pushed, we recognize that we are being triggered. Being aware of your button will train you to be mindful of your reactions.

3. We can avoid anyone or anything that may push our buttons, which is virtually impossible to maintain as a long-term solution, and unhealthy, because we need to be responsible for our triggers in order to be liberated from them. We can only know how far we have come through the echo of the external forces.

If we do not identify our buttons, we will continue to project our pain onto others, damaging our relationships and significantly compromising our lives. Projection and transference are the leading cause of continued hostility among us. Since the world is one massive projection, we need to be careful not to get lost in it.

How to identify your buttons

> We all have unidentified buttons that push us over
> the edge. Once pressed, we go into a mental
> and emotional blackout. Within the darkness,
> we throw punches at anyone, who happens to
> be in our way at that particular moment.

1. Observe your reactivity pattern. Do you get easily triggered? Do you feel easily slighted and disrespected by others? Do you have a tendency to feel shameful, unworthy, abandoned and betrayed?

2. Paint as many circles as the buttons you recognize in yourself. Take each one, and question the dialogue it is telling you. Ask, what false beliefs have I adopted due to these buttons?

3. Write down any disempowering beliefs, and rewrite them in an empowering way. For example, if you feel easily slighted, instead of interpreting that others do not respect you, write down that no one can do so without your consent. Then ask yourself, if you are the one disrespecting or judging yourself.

MORE OFTEN THAN NOT, it will be the case. When you fully accept who you are, you will not feel vulnerable to insults. You do not have to internalize what people say to you, or about you.

4. Dive deeper into the initial cause of your button. Sit down with the emotional pattern that has been created as a result and have a conversation. What we do not acknowledge, doesn't leave us. So make sure to have a talk with it, thank it, and bless it, then ask it to leave, and it will. It may take more than one meeting, but eventually, you will succeed. Once we heal and forgive our first wound, all others go away on their own, because you are no longer a fertile ground for them to grow in.

Core wounds are addressed in later chapters.

Emotional Triggers

> Regardless of who's holding the gun, only you can
> pull the trigger.

Triggers are others' actions and words that cause our old buttons to be pressed. When we are triggered, our reactions are exaggerated and not appropriate to the situation at hand. Because these buttons are linked to and conditioned by past painful experiences, we lose our objectivity and transcend time. We react to the past through this moment.

We may not be able to prevent others from pushing our buttons, but we can prevent them from triggering us. What others push is on them; being triggered is on us. Sometimes, people aren't aware they are triggering you. It is not their responsibility to read you mind. If we communicate to our loved ones, and ask them to refrain from doing so, we might be surprised at how simple it is to avoid conflict. Those, who ignore your request are doing you a favor. When we take it upon ourselves to heal our wounds, we will be less reliant on what others do. This is authentic power. Our triggers are here to point out the work we still have to do, and weed out those, who show lack of respect for your boundaries and process. Communicating honestly will reveal who the genuine people in your life are. Those, who use your buttons against you, do not deserve to know you on a deeper level. Not everyone can be trusted with your vulnerabilities. Test people's trustworthiness in a less risky way. Share a small vulnerability with someone, and watch what they do with it. This may sound cut-throat, but if you communicate with a person that poking you makes you annoyed, and they take that as an opportunity to annoy you further, then this person should not be trusted with deeper vulnerabilities. At times, we will get triggered by unsuspecting people. In this case, it is our absolute responsibility not to blame them for it. When you take responsibility for your core wounds, you will no longer be at the mercy of external factors. It's liberating and empowering when you stop projecting your pain on those, who did not inflict it upon you in the first place.

 "If you do not heal from what hurt you, you'll bleed on people who didn't cut you." ~Author Unknown

Most Toxic Emotions

Show me a disease you want to heal, and I will
show you what you need to forgive.

Fatal illnesses are often rooted in unhealed and unforgiven emotions. Not everyone wants to heal. We are beginning to link physical illness with how we feel. After all, everything is interconnected. Separating things prevents us from healing. Medications may suppress disease, but it doesn't cure it unless we tend to other aspects that are playing a lead role in its manifestation. One of the medical doctors I highly recommend listening to, is Dr. Gabor Maté. His teachings cover the medical tools we can use within the spiritual and emotional realms. From my non-medical point of view, I am offering some examples of physical illnesses and the emotions that may have birthed them:

- High blood pressure: Anxiety/fear of losing control.
- Cancer: Grief/Lack of forgiveness.
- Auto-Immune Disease: Fear of losing autonomy.
- Addiction: Lack of connection /Feelings of unworthiness.
- Narcissism: Self-loathing/Fear of being rejected.
- Psychopathy: Feeling unsafe/Fear of betrayal/Ostracism/Mother Wound.

- Borderline: Fear of abandonment/Fear of love.
- Histrionic: Feeling unseen/unheard/Fear of being irrelevant.
- Heart Disease: Loss/Heartbreak. *(Note: Broken Heart Syndrome leads to Heart Disease)*

Forgiveness, gratitude, and trust are sturdy anchors in our healing journey. With acceptance and self-awareness, we begin to remove the mental roadblocks and release our fears.

SHAME

> Our worth is inherent, and; therefore, is never on the negotiation table.

Shame is a violent, spiritual assault against others and ourselves. It attempts to eradicate someone's worth. Everyone is worthy under divine law. No matter how big the mistakes you've done, your worth cannot be part of the equation. You can lose your social value, but not your worth. The tape of shame is defining someone as a mistake. It does not separate the person from their behavior. We all make mistakes. Surely, some are bigger than others. Some are detrimental. Sometimes someone's actions irreversibly impact someone else's, as is the case in murder. Everyone has to answer for what they have done. But that does not always mean they have to answer to us. We do not have the right to hold them hostage to a mistake, forever.

Your past does not have to be a life sentence, especially when it does not involve a crime against another. I am specifying crimes against others because every culture has its own set of rules. A crime in one culture may be accepted or reversed in another. Anyway, even murderers deserve to be treated with dignity, while behind bars. I know it is a tough thing to accept.

But what would be the point of rendering ourselves into the same monsters we are attacking? We all deserve forgiveness and dignity. This means, you preserve yourself the right to hold on to your own dignity, and refusing to become bitter. We live in a shame culture. The more pain people feel, the more likely they are to point the finger outward. We are either harsh on other people, while taking it easy on ourselves, or vice versa. The theme here is, we rarely have an accurate perception of ourselves and others. So, to use shame as a weapon based on questionable perceptions is in itself a serious crime against humanity. It is such an arrogant judgment as though to say the Universe made a mistake.

> We have a tendency to sum up someone's entire
> character by one truth. We define their lives in
> one mistake. We condense their entire story in
> a word.

It is time to release the toxicity. Give yourself and others a much-needed break. Allow people to grow and create a positive change. It is thanks to our mistakes that we learn. Don't try to take away anyone's dignity. You cannot do so without denying yourself your own. This is a spiritual hostage situation.

One of the common behaviors that boggle my mind is how malicious people can get on social media. They pounce like hyenas on an opportunity to publicly humiliate and shame someone. Instead of addressing their feelings about someone's behavior, they, instead, target an individual with the sole intention of taking them down. Often, I see people celebrating the murder of someone or a group that they oppose. What sets us apart from a murderer, when we are celebrating his death? I remember people celebrating the death of a former president just because they opposed his fanatic views. They reacted in an equally fanatic manner. They didn't feel he deserved to die with dignity. They were beating a dead horse. It is much like a fanatic atheist waging war against a religious fanatic. We see this kind of behavior on a smaller scale in our daily lives; a cocaine addict shaming an alcoholic, and an alcoholic shaming the gambler. Shame is deeply embedded within us. It is cancer to our conscience.

It is a dangerous act of dehumanization, which is the basis for all kinds of evil acts in the world. When you tell someone enough times that they are an unworthy mistake, they will start to believe it. The wound of shame will bleed over every corner of their lives. You will see evidence in it through turning to crime, promiscuity, drug abuse, and abusive relationships. It takes divine intervention to save them from a life of ruin. This can be you, or your loved ones. But it doesn't have to stay this way. We are all worthy of a reprieve.

COMMON PLACES WE EXPERIENCE SHAME:

AT HOME: Parents have historically been shaming their children when they mess up. The message the child receives is that they are only conditionally accepted, and therefore, not inherently worthy. Their worth becomes the prize they have to pay for, and the currency is compliance. Healthy parents separate the behavior from the child. They punish when needed, without withdrawing their love and affection. This does not mean that the parents, who use shame to have control over their child are bad parents, or have malicious intent. It is extremely challenging to raise a child. Parents are humans too, who make mistakes, poor judgment calls and missteps. They are prone to emotional exhaustion that results from raising children. However, I am offering an insight into how the child can internalize the shame, which can be detrimental to their life when they grow up. In extreme cases, it can be detrimental to the parents' lives too. A small shift can save the family from unnecessary heart-ache. Refrain from using your love as a bargaining chip, no matter how major the setbacks and disappointments.

It is especially intensified in a chaotic home environment, where favoritism is present. A parent assigns roles, where one is the golden child and the other, the scapegoat. The roles can be interchangeable if the parent has severe narcissism. Both, the golden child and the scapegoat, feel shame. The former feels they have to be perfect to be worthy, while the latter feels unworthy regardless of how good they are. If the parents abandon their children, one may be bullying the other, because there is no one to instill order or offer protection. Bullied children often attract bullies in other places, such as school, and later attract abusive partners.

AT SCHOOL: How many times have you been shamed in class for being bad at a subject? It is common for teachers to single out one student and shames them for not having the answers, a fulfilled homework, a good mark, or failing to be on time. Other kids learn to shame and bully each other by mirroring the adults. In almost every class there is the scapegoat and the leading bully. It is quite similar to the dynamic of chaotic home environments. Sometimes, the child that is bullied in the home, becomes the bully at school. Other times, they continue to attract bullies to them. The ones doing the bullying have learned somewhere, usually the home, that aggression is the only way of self-protection. It becomes normalized. Schools must take a serious initiative for no bullying tolerance, whether by the students or by the teachers.

. . .

At Work: I wish I could tell you the bullying dynamic and shaming behaviors end with school, but they continue just the same in our professional environment. The difference is, the stakes are much higher. Bullying people at work can take a serious toll on their overall performance, which will impact the entire organization. I have witnessed many great people, who are highly skilled, get sick due to being a target of bullying and shaming from their bosses and colleagues. In extreme cases, they suffer a loss of income, and can barely sustain themselves. This is evident in the state of the world today. We are mostly run by psychopaths, who occupy professions they are not necessarily the best at. Narcissists will exchange you with their shortcomings for your credit. When things go wrong, they will blame those, who worked the hardest, but when it succeeds, they will assign themselves all congratulations. A sociopathic boss will create conflict among the employees rather than ensure harmony. Divide and conquer is the only way to control and destroy. The sooner you recognize this dynamic in your work place, resign, now. It will cost you a lot more, if you stay. These types have no problem destroying themselves, if it is the only way to destroy you.

How to Heal Shame

> When you feel the thorns popping out of your
> face, you know you are going through the labor
> pains of releasing shame.

Identifying your bodily sensations that correspond with your emotions is a great way to gauge your progress. You regain your memory by using sensory memory as described in Chapter 2. It is easy to identify embarrassment by how our face turns red. The blood flows upwards when it comes to all levels of shame. Write down how shame makes you feel in your body. Then write down the experience you can remember when you felt this way for the first time in your life. You should be able to identify what your shame story was, and what false beliefs did you internalize about yourself. The final step, which can be a long process, talk to yourself as you would talk to your child or someone you love. When we talk from this perspective, we become kinder and loving, which is exactly what you need. Whenever possible, surround yourself with ones you trust, who love and value you. Talk to them about your shame when you are ready. When you speak it into an empathetic space, you truly heal. If you choose to share your story on a wide platform, make sure you have already healed, and have the intention to act as a beacon of light to others. How many rape survivors helped lessen the stigma by openly talking about it? However, your safety and mental health must always come first. Mindful sharing is advised to avoid re-traumatization.

ENVY

> Someone's great blessing has sprung from a pain
> that you may not be able to endure. So, envy
> not the blessings they have unless you are
> willing to take on the curses too.

I believe there is a blessing with every individual's name on it, waiting to be received. But because it comes with a price of blood, sweat, and tears, many find it easier to wish away someone's blessings rather than sacrificing for their own. The thing is, it is an endless cycle for the envious among us. If their prayers are answered and their target loses everything, they may feel temporarily satisfied, but soon enough, they will find another target. Their own life gets drained into other people's lives. Being stagnant is not possible.

If we are not moving forward, we will move backward, because we become irrelevant. We are made of energy. Many of us rightfully fear the energetic power of envy. The saddest part is, when we fear it, we begin to almost exclusively share our bad news to protect ourselves. We hide our blessings from others. We begin to hex ourselves with negative mantras and complaints. It is draining. When you sink into this space, your blessings begin to move farther and farther away from you. You manifest what the envious person wanted.

Misery does love company. A better option would be to choose your friends with caution. Not everyone has to hear about everything in your life. Whenever you find yourself descending into negative talk with a specific person, simply remove yourself from the situation altogether. Soon enough, they will forget you, and shift their focus elsewhere, and hopefully, inwards.

How to stop being envious

If you are the one inclined to feel envious, make it a daily practice to write a list of things you are grateful for. Say mantras that empower you and ask empowering questions to help you figure out how to achieve your own goals. Envying others is a form of self-betrayal, and self-abandonment. You need to shift your focus back to yourself. You, too, deserve to achieve your highest potential. When you do this, you will be raising your vibration, and therefore, becoming an inviting, energetic space for blessings to find you.

Ask: What do I want for my life? What are the best methods to achieve my goals? Who do I need to become to be worthy of receiving my blessings? How can I be ready and receptive?

. . .

JEALOUSY

> Jealousy will hit you like a ton of bricks when you
> have a scarcity mentality.

It is falsely believed that all those, who experience jealousy, are lacking in self-confidence. This is only one part of the story. You can feel jealous when you come from a place of lack. Scarcity mentality says there isn't enough for everyone to go around. Abundance says, there is. If you go from rags to riches, you may feel jealousy when someone makes more than you. In your mind, you think, if the other person has it, then I can't have it. The most significant area we experience jealousy is in our relationships in general, and in our romantic relationships in particular. We grew up believing there is only one partner for each of us. Historically, it was detrimental to our survival to choose the best partner. We could not afford to share that partner, because that means resources will have to be divided. In the case of women, it was the only way to know whose child she is bearing. Then there are concerns about preserving the DNA of the family, which was common among Ancient Egyptians and is still alive in some cultures today. Speaking of today, we still carry these memories and fears. No matter how much the world changes, and progresses, our primal fears often drive us.

Here are a few more root causes of jealousy:

1. Being abandoned as a child. Feeling unworthy/unlovable.

2. Being a child of divorce.

3. Having been betrayed in the past.

4. Insecurity about not being the strongest or the most capable to provide.

5. Your partner is a narcissist and is intentionally making you insecure.

6. Social pressure on getting married.

How to Combat Jealousy

To combat anything, first, we need to identify the tape it is playing, and then questioning it. If jealousy's tape is saying, "You are unlovable" or "You lose value, if you are single," question it and remind yourself that you are valuable in your own right. It is wonderful to have someone to share our lives with, but when done to extract value, it becomes empty and unfulfilling. Many people stay in an unhappy marriage for the sake of image. They sacrifice their joy in the name of status. Children get damaged by witnessing their unhappy parents sitting in a loveless marriage more than children of divorced parents, who treat each other with love and mutual respect. Whether you want to be in a partnership or not, make sure it's for a positive reason.

WHEN JEALOUSY IS TRIGGERED by fear of abandonment:

IF JEALOUSY SAYS, "EVERYONE LEAVES ME," then write down the names of the people in your life, who never abandoned you. Take note; though, that the only way we identify with abandonment is by abandoning ourselves. So, even if everyone else left, make sure you do not join them by walking out on yourself. Self-abandoned is a manifestation of early abandonment. Later in life, it is the precursor for others leaving you. Make it your intention to hold on to yourself, regardless of who stays or leaves. When you have your own back, you will carry yourself better. You will not intoxicate or harm yourself, and you won't tolerate abuse of any kind, including the self-inflicted. Jealousy has this way about it, where we devalue ourselves while idealizing our partner and the one we think they cheated with. A jealous mind can be a paranoid mind. Ask yourself, "How am I devaluing myself?", "When was the first time someone devalued me? Who was it?" After you look into yourself for clues, and the answers come to the surface, shift your focus on your partner, and ask, "In what way am I idealizing my partner?", and "What is the accurate perception?" The point is to gain an objective perception of yourself and others. The monkey brain will overwhelm you with all kinds of lies, and this is the way to keep them in check.

A MANTRA:

> My worth is not tied to someone's presence. My value comes from within. It is not at someone else's mercy or charity. I honor and respect myself.

BITTERNESS

> Over-chewing of toxins leaves a bitter taste on our tongues. We will do anything to get rid of it, so we spew it onto others.

How many decades will you waste replaying old tapes?
Bitterness over a past betrayal is poison to the soul. It is a paralyzing agent. The world keeps on moving, leaving the bitter behind. There is no value in this emotion. The irony is, our bitterness is directed at those, who once betrayed us, while we continue to betray ourselves by letting it rob us of our present and future, which makes us more bitter. It is critical to confront yourself if you don't want to waste your life away. It is quite painful to admit to self-betrayal, but it is most dangerous not to put a stop to it. The longer you stew in your bitterness, the more it intensifies.

· · ·

HOW TO RELEASE BITTERNESS

Avoid the cycle of self-abuse. We all betray ourselves sometimes. Remaining remorseful will only waste more time. Use the remorse as an opportunity to end this cycle now. Speak to yourself gently, and applaud yourself for this difficult task. Ask for forgiveness from yourself, and take steps to break this pattern. Create a new habit. Reconnect with your dreams. As long as you are breathing, it is not too late to follow your calling. It takes about 30 days to create a new habit. Take the time to make it up to yourself. Practice self-care. Eat healthy food. Move and exercise. Dance. Write down your intentions. Create goals, and get through them. Keep them achievable. Before you know it, you will be leading a much healthier life. When we take care of ourselves, we attract the right people into our lives, who are willing to help us. Become useful for others. There is nothing more healing than an act of service. It replaces all bitterness with a sweet taste for living.

ANTICIPATION

Anticipation breeds anxiety.

This may come as a surprise to many, but anticipation is an unhealthy emotional state. In fact, it is horrifying. When we sit in anticipation, even for a pleasurable event, our anxiety rises by the minute. Time doesn't move fast enough. The danger of this emotion is that it releases our stress hormones. It messes up with oxytocin, the trust/love hormone because we are in anxiety. Dopamine, the feel-good hormone, is responsible for the anticipation of pleasure, but not pleasure itself. The dopamine levels become significantly high, which increases anxiety. Adrenalin spikes, too, with no outlet. All you have to do is sit and wait.

You may feel it's been 30 minutes when it's been only 5. You then rock back and forth, fidget, shake your leg, move around looking for anything to do, but it still escalates. When the moment finally arrives, it feels like someone gave you a shot of morphine. Anticipation acts like a drug addiction, except it is one you cannot silence by purchase. Due to the intense rollercoaster it takes you on, you become uncomfortably underwhelmed once the anticipated moment finally arrives. Narcissists know the power of anticipation and use it against you. They make you feel uncertain; they make you wait. Then, magically, they become the morphine you are hooked on and think you cannot live without. What is more dangerous about it is that anticipation is the driving emotion behind motivation. Under its hold for prolonged periods of time, you begin to act crazy and make the worst judgment calls. Remain grounded, because you truly will need an anchor to avoid this emotion. To avoid the damage of anticipation, we must make sure not to place a higher value on the object or subject of our desire more than the value we place on ourselves and the present moment.

USEFUL EMOTIONS THAT BECOME TOXIC AS HOME EMOTIONS

GUILT & REMORSE

> Guilt can turn into a wasted emotion quite quickly. It does not serve any purpose, if not followed by a rectifying action.

If you feel guilty about your actions, simply take steps to correct the behavior, apologize if you need to, and do not repeat the offense. Guilt and remorse have two useful functions:
1. We acknowledge the damage we caused to others.

2. We recognize the negative behaviors we need to stop repeating.

What is the point in feeling guilty and sinking into obsession over what you should have done or said or failed to do and say? I remember one of my employees, who had just started work, going into mental paralysis over a mistake she made. I clarified to her that it is ok to make a mistake and that it was expected this early on into her employment. I also requested her not to let guilt block the flow of her work. All she had to do was understand what the mistake was, practice a little more, until she masters the skills enough not to repeat it.

Instead of listening to my feedback, she wasted another week mulling over her mistake to the point that she left all consequent work unaccomplished. Needless to say, I let her go. Her guilt did not do either of us any good. If you feel guilty about something, take steps to make amends.

REGRET

What we fear most is a missed opportunity.

Maybe we didn't express our love enough before someone passed away, or failed to make amends with a lost love. It is not always within our control to avoid regret, but we can use it as a reminder to appreciate people and blessings when we have them. Holding on to regret can only create more to be regretful about. When we deeply regret a past mistake, we have to reach a point of self-forgiveness. Sadly, people have a tendency to continue holding onto the past, which makes it tougher to get out of regret. They think self-forgiveness means betrayal to someone else. It's a useful practice to visualize yourself on your death bed until you know what truly matters. What matters is to make the best out of the life we are given. Regret serves as a teacher to be better and do better. Nobody learns without mistakes. Regret used as a whip; however, will never offer growth or valuable lessons.

> Emotions are beautiful servants, but deadly
> masters.

We have to allow ourselves a second chance because we have a divine purpose to fulfill. Some people go through tragedies that it is unfair to expect them to just get over it. Regret means we haven't fully grieved yet. But even under the most painful circumstances comes a time when we have to turn our regret into a lesson we can appreciate. Whatever the case may be, give yourself time to grieve, but do not make a home of your regrets. I promise it does not make you a bad person for letting it go.

* * *

THE EMOTIONAL GYM

> Emotions are, both, a language and a muscle. They
> need fluency and fortitude.

WE ARE emotional and social beings despite our stubborn belief that we are rational. Our inherent needs for belonging, and connection cannot be ignored. We must fortify our emotional muscles to withstand life's trials. To become well-versed in any language, we must practice it. The emotional gym means taking the time every day to check in with yourself, and how you feel. Be aware of your emotions, and tend to them. Fill yourself up with healthy emotions and energy. It is a form of self-care. Refrain from suppressing the emotions that arise. Notice the people in your life that push you to deny your emotional needs.

Make the necessary changes. It will not serve you to keep emotional vampires around you, who will keep depleting the energy you worked hard to fill. You will find yourself having to keep replenishing what they drain, and soon enough, you won't even have energy for that. Familiarizing yourself with your emotions, you begin the beautiful journey within yourself. This requires sobriety and presence of mind.

EMOTIONAL TRANSITIONS

> The only emotional leap we can take is faith. All
> else needs transitioning.

One of our downfalls is when we feel one emotion, but are expected to express its complete opposite. Imagine the distance between despair and ecstasy. They occupy opposite ends of the emotional scale. We end up "trying" to prove we feel the opposite emotion in overly dramatic ways. For example, if an actor can't contain his joy for landing the role, but the character he is portraying feels grief, he needs to transition gradually towards grief. Otherwise, he makes an effort to show grief by pretending to feel it, and forcing the performance. There is nothing impressive about crocodile tears. The issue is not that the actor can't embody grief, but it's because he was making an emotional leap in a short amount of time, without being fully ready for it. The intention to use easy tears reveals his inauthenticity, because real tears are accompanied by intricate, and involuntary physical reactions such as the quivering of a vein on the temple, a markedly changed posture, and overall energy. Taking an emotional leap is risky when we are forced to use it in our day to day lives. When we are depressed, and pressure ourselves to get out of the depression, we can get easily discouraged. The leap from depression to joy is too great.

Instead, transition gradually without focusing too much on your depression. Make small steps every day. Shift your focus to where you want to be rather than what you are running from. Allow yourself to regress sometimes without judgment. It is more authentic to show emotional fluctuation than to stick to one emotion. We can smile within grief, laugh in the midst of anger, and cry in the middle of joy.

WAYS TO TRAIN YOUR EMOTIONS

1. Write in a journal. Take note of how you feel.

2. Identify your emotional buttons, and take steps to address them one at a time.

3. Understand your emotional triggers. Offer yourself empathy. Forgive yourself, then others

4. Create a list of the boundaries you need in your life & update it as often as needed.

5. List your emotional needs by priority.

6. Next to each need, write what you expect to happen to meet this need. For example, if one of your needs is to be respected, but the conditions that make you feel respected are unrealistic then you will feel easily slighted.

7. Choose one person you feel safe to be vulnerable with. Check in with them and how they feel too. Appreciate each other.

8. Turn your expectations into appreciation. (Tony Robbins)

9. Include something creative in your routine. Dancing is a wonderful way to release emotions. Tango in particular is perfect for that, and has the added components of getting in touch with your divine masculinity/sacred femininity. Flamenco offers power, charisma and confidence.

Emotions are a muscle that is fortified or
weakened by the quality of our thoughts.

CHAPTER 2

THE CHARACTER

Divine Moments of Truth.

Acting is not about pretending. It is a process of authentic Action/Inaction. Actions are the final stage of a thought process. This is how the human mind operates. Even a seemingly thoughtless action is preceded by a thought. It could be an old thought. There is no truly thoughtless action, whether we are aware of it or not; however, it can be mindless. Being mindful is to be aware of the thought. Being thoughtful is taking the time to think it through. The complete immersion into a self creates brilliant moments of involuntary actions. This is especially evident in unforgettable performances. There is a limit to how much an actor can lean on technique. Even if the actor is masterful at expressing their emotions and vulnerabilities, it will not be enough. Sooner or later, the actor becomes repetitive in various roles. They need to develop an ability to transform, both, internally and externally. Adaptability is why actors are called chameleons. They change their true colors with commitment and authenticity.

. . .

THOUGHT PATTERNS

Your life's end result is telling of your core beliefs.

Perspective—>Beliefs—>Perception/Thoughts—>Emotions—>Action/Inaction

ANYTIME YOU WANT to change the bottom line of your life, you can work backwards by looking at your actions, trace them back to the emotion that propelled them, question your thoughts and modify your beliefs by changing your perspective. We must uproot our false/unhealthy beliefs and plant ones that harmonize well with the results we want. We tend to resist letting go of our toxic beliefs, yet keep wishing for better results. Everything is easier said than done, as habits and ancient patterns are tough to break. Still, don't let that played statement become your excuse for not making a timely change.

CHARACTER ANALYSIS

When we know someone's full story, we can no longer judge them. Judgment blocks our understanding.

Approach every character at ground zero; no judgment, prejudice, or assumptions. Observe, with openness and appreciation. Writers and actors do this consistently for their work. They keep their hearts and minds open through consistent introspection. It is a practice many abandoned, which resulted in a mass loss of authenticity. Authentic characters make any story worth telling. A character is composed of a set of behavioral patterns. It runs deeper than a caricature.

Your consistent behavior defines your character; whereas odd behavior puts you out of character. To know someone, you need to look at their pattern rather than summing them up by one odd action that does not define who they truly are. People make the mistake of defining someone by one action that is not part of their pattern. The deeper the insight we have into ourselves, the broader our conception of those different from us. In that case, we understand that we simply made different choices than someone else's without forgetting that we are capable of the same actions.

The most common questions are, *"Who am I?"*, and *"Why am I here?"* If we can answer that, anything else becomes possible. The level of your self-knowledge will determine how you present yourself to the world. We learn to make an impression rather than solely let the world make an impression on us. The less you know yourself, the greater the danger. Because if we identify with the projection rather than the projector, we'd lose all control over our lives. When you don't know who you are, you won't know what you are capable or incapable of, what you accept and what you don't, and whom to trust, or whether you can trust yourself. If you know who you are, you will begin to discover why you are here. Your "why" acts as the fuel that keeps you going towards your purpose.

PROJECTOR & PROJECTION

> We either choose to identify with the projector
> that controls the vision, or we identify
> ourselves with the projection. This is the
> difference between creators and victims.

We share a collective consciousness that fragmented itself. We are the fragments that create the whole. But, because we are part of the higher consciousness, we participate in its creation. When we disconnect from the collective, we feel alone, and powerless. The degree of our inner peace, or lack thereof, depends on how integrated or fragmented we are; the greater the fragmentation, the greater the psychosis. If an entire society is fragmented, they create a shared psychosis. To find well-being, we need to set out to reconnect and collaborate with the whole. Being an observer rather than the observed, we notice the growing distance between who we are, and our thoughts/projections. We find the power to change the picture. External events no longer control or define us. An observer is not taken in mindlessly. Actors have a useful practice, and that is, resetting to their observer selves, and from there, they watch the projection of their character and let themselves be devoured by it. Actors become the embodiment of their vision. When the role is fulfilled, they reset once again, then get ready for the next. However, a highly skilled actor can walk in and out of a given projection on command. This happens by mastering one's thoughts, training one's emotions, intuition, and consistent expansion of one's consciousness.

> That which has no audience loses its power. That
> which is powerful does not need an audience.

Asking "Who am I?" is too broad to answer. I find working our way backward simplifies the process. "Who am I not?" is much easier. Working by omission is effective. Most people know what they don't want, yet have trouble figuring out what they do want. It is a good exercise to get to know yourself, what you want in life, in relationships, etc., by knowing what you don't want or tolerate, so you get to recognize your boundaries. Keep it as an exercise, but not a habit. Often, we get trapped in fighting what we don't want that we end up inviting it. When we don't know who we are we end up projecting on others, while introjecting how they define us. We risk imprisoning others in our projection and losing ourselves to theirs. The observer is impacted by the observed just as much the observed is impacted by the observer.

PROJECTION VS. INTROJECTION

> Anything, and anyone, that is observed, changes with every observer. The meaning the observer attaches to what they are observing is what defines it for them; it is not an absolute truth of that thing or person.

Have you ever been falsely accused of being dramatic by someone, who is dramatic? It is frustrating when people assign to us their negative traits. We are all guilty of that to some degree. Our level of self-awareness and self-deception determine how intense our projections are. It is equally dangerous to project our own good qualities on someone, who does not have them. This invites abuse. Introjection, on the other hand, is when we internalize others' projections on us that we begin to believe it. This is an invitation for gaslighting. How much we know ourselves, and how confident we are, determine whether we buy into others' opinions of us or not. The danger of being prone to introjection is that we attract those who prey on vulnerabilities. Predators can smell the scent of a weak sense of self. Abusive partners often control their victims by using their gullibility and empathy against them. While abusers' mindless projections are powerful, they often consciously choose what they will project on their target to mold them. They can see through the cracks of your identity and hit you where you are at your weakest. For example, if you believe to be ugly, they will call you ugly. They know what you will introject, and what you are less likely to. As time goes on, you become a walking shell, prone to internalize what you previously wouldn't have.

This is when you have crossed over to introject everything they said to you. They chip away at your sense of worth and identity down to the bone. The world reverberates to you what you are already telling yourself about yourself. If you develop a healthy sense of self, you become invulnerable to others' opinions of you. Only then, can you stop watching what they put on their screens, which makes them lose their power over you. We do become what we consistently witness and what we continuously get subjected to.

* * *

CHARACTER OBSERVATORY

Observe without bias. Remain grounded.

When we observe people from a place of appreciation as we would a tree or a lovely child, we become open to receiving them fully. We allow them to tell us who they are without projecting our ideas onto them. You can try it by observing yourself. It will help you gain objectivity when you step out of your head. Take notes on any shifts in your perception. Working through the list backward helps us trace back where others are coming from.

IT IS EASIER to observe an action or notice its absence than to know what someone's motivations are. Intuition, when nurtured, can offer insights regardless of what we see; however, most of the time, we judge the action and stop there without considering the full story. We can judge a woman for stealing, but understand when we find out she had three children to feed. A drug addict is often blamed, but when we know he was subjected to tremendous pain, we empathize.

There is always more to what meets the eye.

* * *

ACTION/INACTION

The action we do not take is equally impactful as
the actions we do take.

Our actions are propelled by the energetic intensity of our emotions. When we observe people's actions and notice an energetic power accompanying it, we become mesmerized. When that same action is empty, we are left unimpressed. An action with a lack of authentic emotion behind it does not leave an impression on us. Meaning, it does not inspire a reaction out of us or within us.

Absence of action can trigger our anxiety because we programmed ourselves to only understand what we see. Failing to act can be a relief following a threat, or a disappointment following a promise or an expectation. When someone doesn't act, we immediately assume they had no real emotion or intention behind the situation. In the face of crisis, some people freeze, and some people see something you deem simple as a crisis, like offering an apology or telling the truth.

When we make a promise, we must be mindful of our emotional engagement. If we genuinely feel a positive emotion about something, we become able to fulfill our promise and follow it with effortless action. If we don't feel like we want to do something, yet promise to do it in the future, we rarely follow through. If we do follow-through, it feels heavy with emptiness, because we do so begrudgingly. Many actors worry about how they will fulfill a certain action on the screen, not realizing it's the emotion they need to feed, and the energy they need to lead with. This will take care of the action or inaction. Once fully integrated with their character, the physical action or inaction will come out naturally. Even inaction will be full of life. Most of the time, we are in a state of reaction. When we feel an emotion, but don't show it to others, we are still reacting. The difference is, we internalize them. We keep it hidden for our protection, but others can still sense it. Every cell and fiber within us is in constant reaction or response to life.

REACTION VS. RESPONSE

> A reaction reveals our conditioning. A response reveals what has been healed.

A reaction is an answer to external actions. It is our autopilot. A response comes from our mindful, and intentional space.

When we react, it is a mindless reply according to what we have been conditioned or triggered by. When we allow our buttons to be triggered by an external event, we go into an autopilot reaction. When we respond, we can reply to others without being phased by them. We feel grounded. This is authentic power.

Being in a state of reaction is much more common because most of us are being led by our shadow/ego selves. Self-responsibility gives us the ability to respond. We cannot be responsible while being in a state of reactivity. Either we respond, or we react.

What we react to reveals what our insecurities are, and what we identify with. It announces our fears. What we respond to, reveals what we have accepted within ourselves, or what we do not identify with.

ENERGY, INTENSITY, AND VIBRATION

> Divine language is energy. No words, action or prayer would be heard without its vibrational match.

People's energy is their first impression, regardless of how they behave and what they say. Everything you ask for is always what you find. It is not your words or actions that create life's reply, but the vibrational energy that carries your words and actions. Check your energy, and check the energy of your goal. Align yourself energetically with it, and then bring it to life through words and action. Your emotional energy can act as your GPS to know the distance between you and your goals. Everything is made of energy. No matter how much you say, wish, claim, or try to do, you will not create the results you want unless you rise or fall to meet it.

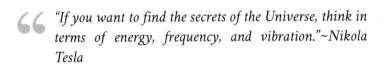 *"If you want to find the secrets of the Universe, think in terms of energy, frequency, and vibration."~Nikola Tesla*

EMOTION

> E-Motion is Energy in Motion. Master your
> emotions to master your energy, both, inner
> and outer.

Where there is an emotion, there is an action; where there is none, there is inaction. Actions are equally taken internally as they are externally. Sometimes, our actions are internal. Directing energy towards someone is still an action. The less we feel, the weaker the action becomes. When we set our minds to do something, we find a way to do it by feeding our emotional fuel towards it. People, who are in touch with their emotions are full of life. They are fully engaged and engaging. Imagine someone giving a speech that puts you to sleep versus someone, who is alive and full of passion. They motivate and inspire us. In love, we come to life; whereas, in a relationship that lost its passion, we become lifeless. It shows in our eyes. When we are radiating, people know we are emotionally fulfilled. We look younger and vibrant. We are lit. When we are not fulfilled, we look dimmed. It's as though we added a decade to our lives.

Abusive relationships will suck the life out of us. Unfulfilled goals and dreams make us bland. It is lights out for us. Being emotionally blunted is painful. When we feel devoid of emotion, it hurts us more than being able to feel our pain. This is because negative emotions still make us connect with our humanity and existence. But not feeling anything at all, we become lifeless. We don't do anything at all. We feel like zombies.

Psychopaths carry much pain due to their emotional void. It is pain of a different kind; one that cannot be filled. So, there is pain that spells life, and pain that makes us dead inside. Have you ever felt a hole in your heart that resulted from extreme pain? The very awareness of that void becomes all that you feel. It happens when we lose someone we love. We then go on to fill the void through substance abuse, and other forms of destructive habits. When we finally hit rock bottom, we wake up once again. Psychopaths live in a space of perpetual lifeless pain. This is why they need to inflict it on others, just to feel alive by proxy. They are unable to stop causing harm because it is the closest way to experience being human. If they cannot create their own emotions, they create it in you, to experience it through you. It becomes an addiction.

The rise in Narcissism and sociopathic behavior is a direct result of decades, if not centuries, of emotional suppression. When we suppress our emotions for long enough, they turn into monsters, hell-bent on consuming our lives whole.

The conditioning that our emotions are something to be ashamed of made us breed personality disordered children. They lead with their Shadow and bring darkness upon us. Once we bring this into the light of awareness, the shadows may begin to disappear.

> The most vital aspect of emotions is to understand
> the thought process that landed us in them, and
> the damaging beliefs that turned them
> against us.

Thoughts

Every emotion begins with a thought.

While we must tend to our emotions to keep them at bay, we must be mindful of the thoughts that are responsible for our emotional state. Thoughts create patterns. The more you think of something, the more powerful it becomes. Every manifestation begins with a thought. The more intense the thought, the more likely it will manifest. Take a color pencil to a piece of white paper. Begin coloring a small circle lightly. Then keep coloring over it. The color intensifies. This is how thoughts operate.

THE THOUGHT you feed is the one that will dictate your emotions, which will lead to your actions. This is why it is important to be mindful of our mental process because it becomes our mentality and state of being. The people you spend the most time with will eventually prompt your thoughts. If I tell you not to think of elephants, I just forced you to think of elephants.

Surround yourself with people, who keep complaining, and paint a dark view of the world, and your thoughts get tainted with dark tones. When you surround yourself with inspirational people, they color you lighter. This is what we mean when we say someone showed us their true colors.

> People's true colors are created by their thought
> patterns.

We live in a time with a shocking rise in sociopathic narcissism. This is largely due to prolonged mass thought control. Any ideology that promotes blind faith, conditions you to suppress your thoughts, eradicate your critical mind, and blunt your emotions will change your brain structure.

Ignorance breeds sociopathy.

Julius Caesar knew what he was doing when he burned The Great Library of Alexandria to the ground. Eradicating education makes us prone to mind control. What they didn't account for; however, is the tyrannical retaliation of those, who were forbidden to learn and think.

The most formidable enemy is one, who is stupid, ignorant,

and sociopathic. This enemy is thoughtless to a degree that they can harm themselves just to harm you. Think of suicide bombers. We can certainly not trust or predict the next move, for they, too, are blind to it. These enemies are not calculating. They are unpredictable and impossible to reason with. Attacking our enemies' education will turn against us in ways we cannot afford or outlive.

PERCEPTIONS

> Every change you seek comes from a shift in your perception.

Reality changes with every perception. What you perceive is what you find. To change your reality, you must make a shift in your perception. The mind is a powerful medium. If you perceive the world as vicious, your mind will look for evidence of viciousness. If you perceive the world as friendly, your mind will find evidence of friendliness.

THERE IS a Buddhist quote that says,

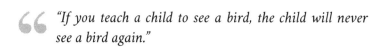 *"If you teach a child to see a bird, the child will never see a bird again."*

What this means is that everything in existence is beyond the labels we give them. But when we imprison things within the confines of a label, we miss out on seeing all of its other dimensions and truth. Every situation in your life can make you happy or sad based on how you look at it. Some people believe that life is a comedy; while others believe it to be a tragedy. It is the same life. It is the constant and we are the variables. Finding humor in a tragic situation is the beginning of healing and reconciliation.

Comedy is tragedy inside out.

We look at the world through our limited perception. We live in a world of duality, where one thing cannot be known without its opposite. But within the duality, there are degrees, and colors, and mysteries. Dualistic views trapped us in black and white thinking. We are swinging between mania and depression. Neither extremes hold the whole truth, not even when they are combined.

When you can tell your traumatic story with humor, know that you have healed. One of my favorite exercises I like to offer my students is to write about something tragic in their lives and find the humor in it. We make it as ridiculous as possible. This is to train our minds to be flexible in the way it perceives events, people, and ourselves. If reality is reliant on your perception, then you have the power to respond to life in a new way. The scenario shifts and the pressure will elevate. You will no longer be possessed by one extreme or another.

Now, you are fluid, and fluid is impossible to bind.

BELIEFS

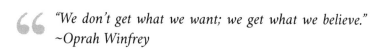

"We don't get what we want; we get what we believe."
~Oprah Winfrey

What we experience during our formative years creates our belief system. The first three years of our lives are highly impressionable because we have not developed a critical mind yet. When we do not have this filter, everything gets stored directly into our subconscious, which can predict our behavioral patterns and future states of being. As Ms. Winfrey pointed out eloquently here is that our belief must be aligned with what we want. If the subconscious belief is that we are unworthy of love, we will not be able to receive love. If we believe we deserve success, we can be successful. It is easy to want something, but not so easy to remove the resisting belief about it. If you want to know your core beliefs, look for clues in your own life. Observe what is working out and what is not working out. If you are struggling with money, then you most likely have a belief that money is evil, that you are unworthy of it, or that you have a scarcity mentality. Spiritual coach, and author, Iyanla Vanzant said as an explanation to losing her millionaire status, *"I was a millionaire, with a welfare mentality".* She didn't realize she had an embedded belief that money has to be gone before she can receive more. If you are struggling in your relationships, you are probably hosting a negative belief about yourself.

 "Your task is not to seek for love, but merely to seek and find all the barriers within yourself that you have built against it". ~Rumi

PERSPECTIVE

We do not have to see it to believe it. We have to
believe it to see it. Ask any child about it.

We gain our perspective by what we see early in life. An infant slowly discovers the world, wide-eyed, and mystified. As we grow to see more and more of what the world shows us, we are gradually adopting beliefs long before we can interpret them. What we are exposed to, creates the foundation from which we build our lives. Beliefs are instilled by our parents' actions before they tell us anything about life. We believe what we see and normalize it. Children imitate the behavior and the energy of the adults around them. From there, we perceive anything familiar to be good, and anything unfamiliar to be bad. The impact of our upbringing is great; therefore, critical to what kind of people we will become. It can be long-lasting and complicated to unravel, unless we make a conscious effort to unlearn and unfold damaging realities, by adopting a vision that offers healthier beliefs. We may not be in control of what we see as children, but we are capable of choosing what we see now. The point is to remember that we can choose our beliefs by changing our perspective, so we can have and hold our desired visions.

MEANING

> The meaning of everything in life is the meaning
> we give it. Change the meaning and watch life
> change with it.

It is said that an observed thing changes with every observer. Everything responds to our perceptions. It is us, who give meaning to the events and relationships in our lives. The way we each interpret the world is unique. The following example is common and demonstrates how the observed changes based on the observer.

Two women are cheated on by their husbands. One makes it to mean that she is unlovable and worthless. She feels humiliated and discarded. The other one makes it to mean that the relationship had run its course and that he is a spineless man, who does not deserve her. She is grateful to have a good reason to end a loveless marriage. She is looking forward to a fresh start. Both women would feel pain; however, the added pain of self-loathing and humiliation adds suffering to the pain.

You must know what meaning your character attaches to life events, and the meaning they attach to the behaviors of others. How we translate things makes us unique. The meaning we attach to things, is what dictates our emotions about it. The mind is like google. If you ask, "Why is this always happening to me?", the mind might answer, because you are stupid.

It is important to ask empowering questions to receive a useful answer.

1. What is this situation trying to teach me?
2. What meaning am I attaching to this situation?
3. What else could it mean?

What others mean does not have to become what you take it to mean.

OBJECTIVE

 "What I know is a man does what he does because he wants something for himself. What do you want, Jack?"~Sawyer, Lost/J.J. Abrams

We are driven by two mindsets; either by what we want or by what we don't want. We can be driven by a desire or by a fear. It may or may not be obvious. Sometimes the external objective hides a deeper one. Sometimes we think we want something, but we want something else. People may voice an objective, but then do nothing to achieve it. They have another objective that overpowers this one. When you have a goal in mind for success, but you keep procrastinating, the overpowering objective is possibly not wanting criticism. Some men waged wars on entire civilizations for love. We can take drastic measures to achieve something. Some people appear to want to cause you harm, but what they are driven by is their fear of losing something else. Knowing what someone wants, and what they are motivated by, helps us unveil more layers into their character. A writer has to be mindful of these elements, because if it isn't clear what a character wants and what motivates them, then we will never know who they truly are.

FEAR IS the main driver of our desires. We may want marriage in fear of being alone; control in fear of losing someone, or destruction of another in fear of being destroyed. We must have the courage to know what we truly want and to take an emotional risk by asking for it. We have to be willing and prepared for being rejected and denied and to have enough grace to accept it. When fear is replaced with courage, our lives will be consciously directed towards purpose rather than wasted on running from things we fear.

MOTIVATION

> We are motivated by our fears until we put our
> higher purpose behind the wheels. Courage is
> what we need.

Our motivation is the fuel that keeps us moving forward. Knowing why we do what we do or want what we want is what we need to accomplish our goals. When we lose sight of our motivations, we lose our fire, persistence, and consistency. Clarity of our reasons will help us decide on what actions to take and what not to take. The strength and integrity of our reasons define the quality of our results. Sometimes we forget why we set out to do something. All we need is a reminder of the "why" to get back on track. If we have weak reasons, our performance becomes weak, which produces poor results.

If you want to achieve something, but it never seems to be working out, question your motivation behind it. If your motivation to do something is to avoid something else, then you are acting from a place of opposition. It may prove useful for a while, but it won't get you far. What we avoid keeps following us until we deal with it. This is how we can keep our motivations in check. Once we deal with where we have been, we can be free to gas up for where we want to go.

Exercise: Take a pen and paper, and write down your motivations behind a variety of actions. If you notice weak reasons, replace them with stronger ones, or stop the action itself, if it's not useful.

Are you motivated by love or fear?

* * *

SUBTEXT

What we can see and feel, does not need to be spelled out.

The subtext is the truth between the lines. It is the truth we attempt to hide. People naturally hide their emotions, and often, their motivations. Some people are highly skilled at manipulation. So much so, they can sometimes mask their energy.

When actors figure out the subtext, their performance

becomes effortless. Actors know their truth stems from the subtext. Weak actors act out their lines. It is empty.

IT IS in the unsaid and the silent moments that make your character full, honest and relatable. This is what gives life and meaning to words. Words can be easily deceptive. We need our intuition and emotional intelligence to cut through the bullshit. It is an especially important skill to have to avoid being manipulated and deceived.

COVERING THE BASICS

The following is a list of defining factors of an individual. When analyzing someone's character, it is important to bear all these elements in mind rather than sticking to the obvious. A human being is layered and intricate; we cannot possibly understand someone fully without bearing all aspects in mind. The less an actor judges his character, the greater the performance. Positive ignorance is when we transcend our assumptions to be fully receptive to new information. Answer the following about yourself and see how complex a human being truly is.

* * *

BELIEF SYSTEM & PERSONAL EXPRESSION

- Religion/Spirituality
- Lifestyle
- Values
- Chosen Identity
- Sense of Humor
- Physical Appearance/Fashion Sense

- Scars
- Quirks
- Talents

BIOLOGICAL FACTORS & Ancestral Influences

- Genetic Dispositions
- Active Physical Ailments
- Psychosomatic Ailments
- Emotional Patterns
- Spiritual Illness

PSYCHOLOGICAL MAP

- Core Wounds
- Deepest fears
- Psychological Diagnosis
- Past Traumas
- Current State

CHECK-IN WITH YOUR NEEDS, and ask what methods you use to meet those needs. Are there any methods that you assigned to meet a particular need that has proven unhelpful? Do you choose a constructive or destructive way? Is your method empowering or disempowering? How else can you meet your needs that better honors who you are?

Now try to answer the same questions about a character you want to play, or someone you love. You will be surprised at how much you don't know. This is a great way to connect. Prompting our minds to think of something proves how powerful our minds are when directed. When we apply our minds, they can open amazing paths. However, using this technique as an avoidance of something that needs your attention, or as an excuse for being the way you are, without the possibility for positive change, is quite damaging. We do not have to remain enslaved by these elements forever.

Demons confronted are demons no more.

EMBODIMENT

The most powerful people are those, who are emotionally free.

People are happiest when they are emotionally free. There is a powerful presence to those uninhibited by social norms. When we are enslaved by our thoughts and emotions, we look dim. I do not advocate using your inhibitions to oppress others, nor do I encourage being so recklessly uninhibited that we infringe on others' rights, or use it to show scorn. Freedom comes with responsibility.

Actors are blessed with being able to express their otherwise tamed selves without real consequences. Spontaneity is one of the top qualities I look for in an actor and friends alike. The energy becomes fluid and so does creativity. I used to get confused when an actor struggles with **improvisation**, especially when they have all the knowledge they need about the character. Then it hit me. Spontaneity is a quality of the free-spirited. Improvisation requires confidence and to be willing to make a fool of oneself. Self-consciousness is an enemy to a free-spirit. Lack of confidence will compromise your presence.

Self-obsession prevents us from connecting with others. We cannot engage anyone outside of ourselves. Practicing improv can be the remedy, and so is being adventurous. Bland and boring have no place in friendship or love. The embodiment of a character requires you to take a deep dive into the collective consciousness so you can access someone else's. It takes skill to do so safely, and a tremendous amount of courage. Non-writers and non-actors can use the methods of embodiment anytime they want to change their lives, and become a better version of themselves. It can strengthen our connection with our loved ones, as we are able to understand them more deeply, and hold space for them as we do for ourselves. We need to effortlessly shift our energies, and remain open to explore new territories.

> We need consistency to achieve our goals, but we
> need flexibility with our methods.

METHODS TO BEGIN THE PROCESS

1. Decide who you want to be, and be as specific and as detailed as possible.

2. Use mantras, meditation, and visualization of the new character's inner and outer world. Listen to the music that belongs to this character, and play relevant educational videos in your sleep. It is a form of self-hypnosis. This is the cocoon phase.

3. After the cocoon phase, you naturally go through a metamorphosis.

4. As an actor, you don't need to completely abandon who you are, or to act out your character's behavior if it's unacceptable. But be willing to experiment within reason.

5. Free write in the character's voice. Delete anything that comes from your limited ideas. Use this exercise for yourself, except, don't delete anything that comes out.

ARTISTS HAVE a great responsibility of knowing themselves deeply enough to know others deeply. Portrayals of characters must be respected, and not limited to surface level. It is our duty to enrich our lives with experiences that transcend the limitations of our personal history, so we can represent people, who can only be seen and heard through our work. Empathy is the foundation to all forms of education.

EMPATHY

Empathy is critical to the process of embodiment. It is the whole intention of this book. I have known great writers and actors, who are psychopaths and narcissists. They don't have the kind of empathy most people relate to. But they do have it in their own way. Since we have varying degrees of it, and some of us lack it altogether, I will break it down into four categories:

HEALTHY EMPATHY: A natural ability to put yourself in another's shoes, and understanding their psychological make-up without judgment.

SELECTIVE EMPATHY: It is an unintentional occurrence. We can only empathize with what we understand. True empathy is not selective. If it is, then none of it is authentic. The degree of our empathy is proportionate to the degree of our understanding.

. . .

COLD EMPATHY: *The ability to have a symbolic x-ray vision into other people, without connecting emotion to it. This type is intellectual and often predatory. Psychopaths and narcissists can be incredible at deciphering others. They may have a better insight into people because they are not clouded by emotion.*

TOXIC EMPATHY: *When you immerse yourself deeply into someone else's story that you lose empathy for yourself and your well-being. Sometimes we sacrifice ourselves to prove we are good people. But if empathy does not start with ourselves, we force others to be indebted to us. Our help becomes grounds for resentment. It is not empathy at all.*

ACTIVE LISTENING

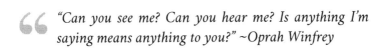 *"Can you see me? Can you hear me? Is anything I'm saying means anything to you?"* ~Oprah Winfrey

Active listening is not limited to hearing someone out when they speak. If we only hear the words spoken, it means we are not engaging in active listening. It is the ability to listen to the energies of people and places; listening to tone, to what is between the lines, the silence; listening to our own intuition, and our bodies. Listening is not an easy skill to have in these times. The world is exceedingly noisy and technology made it even more so. We have become such bad listeners, even to ourselves. We can't hear our own intuition or our bodies. It can be developed; however, if we can mute unnecessary noise. Not everything needs our engagement. Unfortunately, though, while we became bad listeners towards our loved ones and ourselves, it is often due to tuning in to things that drain our energy. We are overwhelmed with junk information, which we don't know how to control. As a result, we tune out the people and things that we can control; unfortunately, they are mostly the people and things that matter most to us. We can't control traffic noise, or people's energies around us all day at work or social events. But we can tell our loved ones to shut the hell up and leave us alone. Underneath this; however, is our fear of being present in an emotional space. It is easy for us to tune in to meaningless noise, because we don't have to emotionally invest in it. We fear that engaging in one emotion will open a sewage within us that we are not ready for. The cost of succumbing to noise rather than investing in what truly matters is much higher down the line, and often, we realize it when it's too late to reverse it.

NOISE TO ISOLATE:

Actors are skilled at tuning out any noise that does not serve a purpose in a given scene. Everyone has this ability; the difference is whether you can do so on command or not. It is a matter of focus. Have you ever been so intensely focused on something that you don't hear someone talking right next to you? Your mind isolates all external noise. To do this on command, all you need to do is train your focus. Identify junk noise, and eliminate from your life what you can. The ones you can't completely eliminate, you can learn to tune them out. Deleting junk information helps a great deal.

- Meditate. Meditate. Meditate.
- Limit social media.
- Create a clear intention before you agree to a meeting. People waste hours in business meetings for something that could have been done by email or a fraction of the time.
- Do not listen to chronic complainers, and gossipers, or tolerate boring conversations just to be polite.

- Do not allow your inner critic to verbally abuse you.
- No TV or Radio without consciously choosing what you are listening to. Mindless listening goes straight into your subconscious.
- Listen to music that inspires and motivates you.
- Be efficient in your conversations. Refrain from going into mental and verbal loops.
- Make time for solitude.
- Have a sense of the energy you surround yourself with. Avoid energy vampires. Limit your alcohol consumption; it kills intuition.

VOCALS

> The less we feel understood, the more we raise our voice.

The world is getting quite noisy. Crowded cities are naturally louder. We can get loud when we are positively, or negatively excited. Some people are naturally loud. Nonetheless, I believe there are deeper reasons beyond that. Sure, the city offers a busy and fast lifestyle that we have less energy to listen to ourselves and each other. Speaking loudly can be a symptom of our fear of being misunderstood. We are suffering from people offloading their reality on us, and we are overwhelmed. The fear of being misunderstood sends a signal to our brain that we are physically distant from each other, and; therefore, we have to yell, even if we are sitting at the same table. When we are surrounded by noise for most of the day, we become conditioned to raise our voice when we want to express something. We bring this conditioning home, even if the home is quiet and we are trying to have a conversation with our partners. We assume they won't understand. I wondered why impoverished areas with little to non-existent education, are significantly noisier. When we are not educated, we cannot express thoughts efficiently and have a hard time analyzing the thoughts of others. Often, we overcompensate our lack of understanding of ourselves by overdramatizing our emotional expression.

Critical thinking is diminished by a lack of education, not only academically, but also spiritually. We can be illiterate, yet have wisdom. Introspection teaches us to master our thoughts so that when we stop thinking, it is to have inner stillness. This is not the type of non-thinking I am referring to here. When we don't think for ourselves, we become less grounded. Since our thoughts create our emotions, our sense of connection is heavily impacted.

There are a few main reasons why we get loud:

1. When we cannot articulate ourselves well, due to not understanding something well enough.

2. When we have no control over our thoughts, and therefore, our emotions get out of hand.

3. Mindlessness in general, as is the case when we are drunk for example.

4. It can be caused by overthinking, intense pain, or intense joy.

5. Lacking intelligence and confidence lead to yelling.

CONFIDENCE AND INTELLIGENCE play a key role in how we express ourselves. When we think of someone with authentic power, we describe them as graceful, articulate, and soft-spoken. Think of the smooth operators we fall for.

Former President Barack Obama and former first lady, Michelle, are a true depiction of grace.

The Godfather never raises his voice. Can you imagine a hysterical leader?

> Those, who cannot master themselves, do not have
> the capacity to lead.

Have you noticed the stark difference between the level of noise between social classes? Or how the less educated we are, the louder we become? How those, who have authentic power speak less, and when they do, they do so in a grounded manner? Do you ever become hysterical when someone refuses to understand you or falsely accuses you of something?

OUR SIGNIFICANT RELATIONSHIPS, being our most sensitive trigger area, bring on more yelling than we dare to admit. The less we care about someone, the less hysterical we become. We are indifferent to their opinion. Yet, the more our ego gets bruised, and the more weak-minded we are, the more volatile we become. Sometimes we scream at strangers because we can't scream at our loved ones. And those, who do scream at their loved ones tend to be softer with strangers.

> Triggering each other into hysterics is inevitable,
> but we can make sure our apologies are louder
> than our moments of disrespect.

We whisper apologies since we are now calm. Some people have a serious problem with the admission of guilt and refuse to apologise altogether. Then, they will blame you for not getting over it, or for being too sensitive. This ended many relationships when all it takes is to at least offer the same amount of effort to make amends as the effort it took to inflict hurt.

Our tone of voice says a lot about our emotions. You can say the same sentence in a variety of tones, and the meaning will dramatically change. Try saying, "Good morning" in many emotional states. Say it happily, sadly, or aggressively. Our tone is more critical than what we actually say. As the old saying goes, *"It is not what you say, it is how you say it."*

THROUGH TONE, we can gauge someone's mood and intention. It is the dividing line between a genuine compliment and a backhanded one. Manipulative people are highly skilled at playing on the tone of their voice. They may say a bunch of senseless words, yet we still get hypnotized by their tone.

THE VOICE: Let your voice come naturally by fully connecting with the appropriate emotion.

THE TONE: Our tone comes from our mood. It changes the meaning of what we say.

THE PITCH: This stems from the intensity of our emotion.

THE MELODY: Everyone speaks in a unique melody. Stay true to the character's melody. It's awful when all characters sound the same, and even more so, when people imitate each other like parrots. Some communities begin to sound uniform when they abandon their individuality. It sounds robotic.

. . .

Words Emphasis: What we emphasize is what is most important for us at the moment. Listen for emphasis.

> Mindlessness and lack of confidence are noisy.
> The powerful have no need to raise their voice.

Voices in your head

Living in a state of perceived crisis, the voices in our heads get louder and less coherent. We get lost in the chaos, trying to focus and understand what we are going through. We see others talking to us as interruptions to the circus we are dealing with inside. The key is to pay attention to which voices you allow to get the loudest. Do you have voices of love or fear? Are you kind or abusive to yourself? Are you solution-oriented, or lost in the maze of circular thinking?

Memory

> Memory is a subjective story. It stems from our
> interpretations of events; therefore, it is not a
> reliable source for truth. We may share aspects
> of memory, but it cannot be fully matched.

An actor has a lot to remember and a lot to forget. They need to remember their lines, and the character's history, first from the actors' point of view, and then from the character's point of view. They have to forget their own emotions and history and embrace those of the characters'. We can make use of those exercises when we want to get over our own memories so we are no longer imprisoned by our history. It serves us well to be selective of what we store in our minds. Forgetfulness occurs when we are overwhelmed with unnecessary information. Once we discard what is needlessly taking space in our mental drive, we become free to focus on what we do need. Forgetfulness has a lot to do with a lack of focus and of presence.

* * *

Memorizing the Dialogue

> *The quality of your focus and the level of your emotional engagement will determine the quality of your memory.*

Unless you had a head injury, or suffering dementia, your memory suffers due to lack of focus, lack of emotional investment, and/or mental exhaustion. We are all becoming increasingly forgetful, because we are mentally drained. Remembering dialogue is at the bottom of my concerns. It is not about repetition, but about engagement.

Spoken communication occupies a small percentage of our overall communication. I am not discounting the importance of dialogue in dramatic work or life situations; however, it shouldn't be prioritized over non-verbal communication. Many actors worry about memorizing their dialogue. While it is a critical part of acting, it can easily damage the performance if it's memorized without using deeper forms of communication. In "real" life, we don't worry about forgetting the lines we want to say to others, unless we are lying.

This is because we know who we are and what we want. We know our history and are able to recall events. Even those with dementia don't sit around worrying about their next line. An actor's job is to know the overall memory for their character and understand what is happening in every given scene. The dialogue will begin to naturally flow without sounding robotic. My suggestion is to leave the memorization for the final stage. First, read the script, if available, for a general idea. Then, read a second time with a focus on your own character and their relationship with others.

THE THIRD READ needs to go at a slower pace, where you break it down as follows:

1. Write down the overall objective and intention of your character. Take note of their home emotions.

2. Break down every scene more extensively. Next to each line, note the following:

1. Emotion. 2. Objective 3. Subtext

4. The energy you embody. 5. The intensity of your emotions. 6. The meaning you give to what other characters are saying.

NOTE: If you want to remember something, attach an emotion to it, a visual impression and create connections through all of your other senses. This is why people with feminine energy tend to have a better memory. They attach emotion. Masculine energy does not, and is; therefore, forgetful.

EMOTIONAL MEMORY

I don't recommend using your own emotional memory or history to invoke an emotion throughout the entire process. Use it as a vehicle to get you closer to the character, and slowly move away from your own reality and into theirs.

For example, if your character is crying over the loss of their spouse, you cannot use your memory of losing a parent. Even if you share an experience with your character, they will cry and grieve differently.

If you use your own history, you may be able to pull it off in a given project, but you will end up repeating yourself in future roles. Your talent will be limited to self-expression and feeling comfortable with your vulnerability. How many actors impressed us once or twice before we realized they are always the same? On the other hand, think of actors who are true chameleons. They are so committed to their characters that we forget who they are as people, and who they were in past roles.

Note: Think of Joaquin Phoenix in Joker versus his embodiment of Johnny Cash in Walk the Line.

SENSORY MEMORY

In order to connect with yourself or a character you want to embody, you have to start with stillness. Meditation helps us identify with being the observer and separates us from the projection. Once grounded and still, you can begin calling upon your senses to help you create a specific memory.

We use our 5 senses until we are transported into the desired memory. By recalling how something feels, looks, sounds, tastes, and smells like, we transport ourselves back fully. Once back, the words will flow naturally, because you are present at that moment in time.

The mind is impressionable and reacts to what you tell it to think about. If you think of your favorite food, your mouth will begin to water. You may call upon a fragrance and instantly be taken back into the moment associated with it. Maybe it was the scent of your late grandmother or a lost lover. With that, your emotions will come to the surface, and your vulnerability will be authentic.

. . .

EXERCISING YOUR SENSORY MEMORY

In city life, our senses have weakened. We can't taste, smell, or feel as we would in Nature. To strengthen them, we need to put them to work. A trained sensory memory can serve us greatly in life. Our intuition guards us against danger, as it also guides us towards the right path. You will no longer feel blocked by your own thoughts, and your actions will be aligned with your essence. This is how actors achieve presence. The performance is no longer forced and you won't need to indicate how you feel. It will flow through you. Trust that the proper responses will emerge once you get mentally still.

Using this exercise for your personal life is equally powerful and necessary. You are free to reinvent who you are. The point is to reach authenticity. When you are integrated, everything else in your life becomes integrated just the same. These exercises are fundamental to grounding and for releasing traumas.

HERE ARE *a few scenarios to use:*

IMAGINE an actor is about to shoot a scene, where he is in a jungle and has to run in tremendous fear from a grizzly bear. There is no bear chasing him, of course, but the character has to believe there is. Most of us are fortunate enough to not have been in this situation.

FOR THE ACTOR; however, he needs to create all of the conditions that would come up as though it were real. Anyone can run in front of the camera. But it takes an active imagination and a highly skilled actor to pull it off authentically without appearing ridiculous. First, find the common ground on which you can relate to the character. We can begin with intense fear; the kind that gets your adrenalin pumping.

THE SCENE REQUIRES the actor to go into Flight Mode. You may begin by recalling the bodily sensation of adrenalin, how your legs can feel like they are flying, your heart racing, your head numbing, and your cells buzzing with a consistent electrical current running through you. You can use meditation to intensify these sensations.

VISUALIZE A GRIZZLY BEAR. Thanks to technology and incredible shows out there, you can turn to animal related documentaries depicting this type of danger. Get lost in it, preferably, before bedtime. You can call upon it in your dreams just the same. How often have you watched a horror movie only to sink into a palpable nightmare? This will allow you to step into the ordeal without having to pretend before the camera. It is now part of your reality.

LET'S say you are lucky enough to shoot on location. You go to the jungle on a sunny day, but in the scene, it will be winter and raining heavily. The way we sweat from the heat is different from winter sweat or perspiration by fear. You have to meditate on the weather.

Now, what if you are shooting in a studio. The heat of the lighting is directly on you. There is a green screen behind you, and a bunch of crew members around you? The more you practice the techniques of memory invocation and active imagination, the easier it will be, even under such tricky shooting conditions.

THE MORE YOU think of something the more likely it will manifest. Everything starts in our minds. You already know how to do this, if you are like most people, who fill their mind with scenarios and fears that create real anxiety within them. We do the same thing when we want to invoke positive emotions when we get lost in our thoughts of pleasant memories, hopes, and dreams.

SELECTIVE MEMORY

Once the actor reads an entire script, they have to block out certain information that is not yet accessible to the character. The shoot is usually non-linear. They may shoot the last scene first, and the first scene after they already shot all of act two. This is where committing to the moment comes into play. The intense focus on the present moment will temporarily delete other memories. We remember what we focus on with emotional engagement.

SUPPRESSED MEMORY

Most of us suppress traumatic memories. It is the mind's way of protecting itself. It prevents a nervous breakdown. Whether it's a good idea to unearth suppressed memories or not varies from person to person, and it is best done with a medical professional or a trusted shaman. To understand how to suppress certain memories for the character, is to create the memory, then actively reject it, and understand how it can impact your behavior in general. A good hypnotherapist can help guide an actor to achieve this.

. . .

MEMORY DISTORTION

Memory is created by perception, which is extremely subjective. It is safe to say that most of our memories are distorted. We either create a memory that paints us as victims or heroes, even if we were, in truth, neither. Your character's perception will determine which memories they distort the most, and how rigid they are in their perception. It will help you predict future behaviors and reactions.

* * *

INTENTIONAL MEMORY LOSS

We can set out to lose memory by changing the meaning of it. Once we change the meaning, we can re-write the story. This is useful when we want to leave a character or our old self behind. We do so by intentionally recording new information into our memory bank. It is worth noting that no memory is ever completely lost from existence. We don't want to eliminate anything here. But there are things that when dealt with, will no longer need to occupy space in our memory bank. Losing memory helps when we lose an emotion we once had for someone or something. Without an attached emotion, we are able to forget and move on.

ACTIVE IMAGINATION

> "If the doors of perception were cleansed, everything would appear to man as it is... Infinite. For man has closed himself up, till he sees all things through narrow chinks of his cavern."~William Blake

Imagination is something we practice all the time. When we hear a story, we create our own vision of it. Our minds are designed to fill in the gaps. Every story has a unique impression. When we daydream, we get involved in the setting and scenarios. It's powerful in the way that we can sometimes get confused if something took place in the outer world or not. We ascertain that something did happen when it didn't.

> Your mind doesn't know the difference between
> what is and what isn't. It believes what you tell
> it, and goes on to materialize it.

Remember when we were children and we would feign a stomach ache to avoid school, and we act it so well that we end up feeling sick to our stomach the rest of the day? This is mind over matter. Tony Robbins teaches this and primes himself and others to such a degree that they walk barefoot on hot coal without feeling a thing. There are gurus and scientists, who teach this concept by controlling their body temperature. They go into ice-cold water and feel fine. A dear friend, *Moses*, tried it for himself. He dives in cold water without a wetsuit, and primes himself to adjust his body temperature to normal, while others are freezing in full wetsuits. An active imagination is the intentional creation of a vision, event, or dialogue. We become the projectors of the story. Our minds can't discern what is real or imagined; the more powerful the imagination, the less the discernment.

What we perceive as unreal is what we cannot achieve. It has been proven that when we consistently feed our imagination and visualization skills that we end up creating our reality, given we don't create resisting beliefs at the same time.

WE STILL HAVE to put in the work. We can't imagine our way into getting our dream job. But when we can see the result we want, and use our imagination with the intention to make it as vivid as possible, our minds begin to bring it into existence. Your behavior begins to change. You will catch yourself smiling with gratitude in response to your vision as though it is already here. The same applies when we train our minds to imagine negative events.

EVERYTHING WE BRING into existence begins in our minds, but it does not make it any less real. "It's only in your head" is a useless and condescending thing to say. It implies the person is crazy, which leaves them feeling isolated and invalidated. What isn't in our heads anyway?

You will see it when you believe it.

Using your capacity for active imagination to create the reality you want rather than the one you don't, will dramatically elevate your standards. You will be more likely to move toward this vision, and have a greater chance at success. If you listen to Basketball players, for example, they see themselves getting a shot in their mind's eye before they actually score it. Martial artists know this all too well. Don't just watch Bruce Lee; listen to what he says about the power of mind.

HERE IS AN EXERCISE. *Give it a shot:*
Get comfortable in a quiet mental and physical space. Close your eyes and imagine something you really want. For this, we will use a dream house as an example. But you can use whatever you want. See the house in detail. Know the location. If it has a garden, what does it look like? Is it an oceanfront? What are the colors, smells, and energies in the house? See the furniture, and use them. You get the idea. Keep exploring it. Before long, you are transported into that house. Notice your emotions and how

your face lights up. Are you smiling? Are you feeling gratitude and peace in your heart?

You can apply this to who you want to become. Visualize yourself as the best version of yourself. What does your hair look like? What is your fashion sense? Are you becoming more elegant, hippy, or like a rockstar? Feel your energy as that self. What would you have achieved in your life? Visualize every single thing about you. When we keep the vision alive, we bring it into our reality. We become the vision. The rules are, we must remove our resistance, cognitive dissonance, and we must take inspired action. Writers, Actors, Musicians, and Athletes, use their imagination all the time. Just like everyone else, they create their reality. The difference is, they consistently put it into practice.

CHAPTER 3
THE SPIRITUALITY OF LIFE

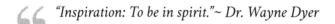 *"We are not human beings having a spiritual experience. We are spiritual beings having a human experience." Pierre Teilhard de Chardin*

Our physical existence is the manifestation of the collective projection. The part of us that is human is a fraction of what we are made of.

In order to fully grasp someone, we must include the greater part of who they are, that is, their spirit. The entertainment field deals with human nature. When we write characters, we cannot discount their spiritual side and their vibrational energy. Artists connect with spirit to be in a state of inspiration. Actors must carry themselves beyond their physical existence. It has to be a natural result of feeding their spiritual presence.

"Inspiration: To be in spirit."~ Dr. Wayne Dyer

CREATIVITY HAPPENS when we connect with spirit. When we define something through a purely mental space, our creativity suffers. All things in the universe require a creative mind. The essence of all things is creative energy. When we connect with our spirit, we access limitless esoteric truth and reach heights and see solutions that we previously couldn't.

THERE IS evidence of our spiritual nature. On a small scale, we identify with energies and intangible concepts such as intuitive messages, love, and moments of genius. We receive accurate information through our intuition without any physical evidence for it. You have a part within that is all-knowing. To tap into it, our minds must be silenced, and our mental barriers must be demolished. We have to open up our minds if we want to be receptive to our inner wisdom.

 "There is a voice that doesn't use words. Listen."~Rumi

CONSCIOUSNESS

Bill Hicks said it best, "There is only one consciousness, experiencing itself subjectively. There's no such thing as death; life is only a dream, and we are the imagination of ourselves."

COLLECTIVE CONSCIOUSNESS

Our collective consciousness is perceived in a million ways and goes by many names. It transcends description. Some of us call it God, Nature, Energy, or Higher Power. How each of us relates to it is subjective. We cannot fully conceive of something objective in a subjective way. Whatever you make of it is personal, yet it fills a piece of its magnificent puzzle. It is what you say it is, and what everyone says it is.

MY HUMBLE KNOWING tells me it is the sum of all parts. It is omnipresent and omniscient. We are part of it and it is within us. It resides in every molecule in existence. Its language transcends words. It has rhythm and song. It is the maestro of our orchestra. It is the source and we are the projections of it. I believe in oneness and unity. Nothing is separate.

Uni-Verse: One Verse. One Song.

Aligning our subjective music with divine music, we experience harmony. Everything flows. Ancient scriptures came into being when people had an abundance of inner stillness and integration. The 99 names describe characteristics that exist in all of Nature, including us. The mysterious 100th name is what encompasses the whole.

I HAD A VISION, where I saw a diamond-shaped piece of sacred geometry. When we maintain the awareness of our interconnectedness, we transcend time and space. We tap into the collective consciousness for more feedback. Suffering is the ego's illusion of our separateness. But when we connect with source energy, we feel home.

The voice said, "Anything that is one is lonely. We need feedback to see ourselves. So it projected itself into billions of beings, who allow it to experience itself subjectively."

Subjective Consciousness

To each their consciousness.

Subjective reality is often confused with truth. We feel separate. We think we are independent of each other. While that may seem true in some respect, it is not.

Our egos promote apartheid; whereas our souls confirm our connection by oneness. In the lovely sketch I made for you below, The three individuals represent us in human form. We have a perceived space between us, which, in essence, is filled with energetic fields and molecules, etc. But, because we don't see them, we buy into the illusion of separation. We get glimpses of them when we feel a connection with someone. Below the three sticks people, are roots like those of a tree. Our roots are connected to our subconscious selves, and each others'. In our subconscious, we are separated by our history and what lies beneath our surface. This is where we confront our respective memories and core wounds. In that confrontation, we begin a process of sorting them out to heal. This is why sharing our stories heals us and others too. Healing is neither linear, nor can we complete it in one sitting. We sort out one core issue at a time, so we can have time to process it. With every session of healing, our patterns become a little lighter. But when we falsely believe that we are done, we land back into our habits, and feel disheartened for revisiting the lesson. We fall through the branch depicted on the right. As the patterns get lighter with time, we manage to raise our vibration. Eventually, when we are done, we ascend out of that loop. We rise into a higher dimension of consciousness.

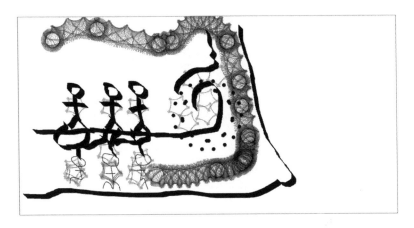

My humble drawing that depicts levels of consciousness and their dimensions.

DESCENSION & ASCENSION

It is impossible to go back to a previous level of consciousness. Once we become aware of something, we cannot sink back in a state of unawareness. It is much like visiting a new country. Once you visit it, you cannot un-know it. Unless we experience memory loss, we will always know this country. Consciousness is the same way. We experience a tremendous disconnect when we try to communicate with others through a consciousness that is different from theirs. We can inspire expansion, but we cannot change someone's consciousness before they are ready for it. Each one of us has their pace. Everything is in perfect divine order. When we raise awareness, we can inspire change, but only in those ready to abandon their old ways. Every stage has its purpose, but we must be willing to let go when it is time.

WHAT IF AN ACTOR has to play a role, where his character hosts a lower or higher state of consciousness than his own? I asked this question to Forrest Whitaker once at his seminar during a film festival. He thought the question was condescending. I understand why it can come off that way, but that wasn't the case. We cannot control the meaning someone assigns to our words. In this moment, his automatic response was based on an assumption, because he doesn't know where I was coming from. We do not know each other. The point of the question is that we all occupy different levels of consciousness. So, how can you embody a character, who is unaware of something, that the actor is, in fact, aware of? How can you host a consciousness that is younger or older than your own? It is a personal struggle for me to write a character, whose intelligence in one area is much higher than my own. The character may be a scientific genius.

WHEN SOMEONE IS EMOTIONALLY manipulative and highly skilled at deception in general, we can often fall for it, because we are not operating from the same level of consciousness. Writing a conniving person is not simple, if you are not street smart. There is always extensive research, inviting another writer to contribute. I chose to go straight to the source, and let them give me a crash course in what they do best. As writers, we have a responsibility to write the characters authentically rather than settle for shallow observations and allow our limited understanding to taint an otherwise interesting character. Some writers want to produce any script, and they end up with a bunch of senseless fillers rather than do the work necessary. It is rewarding to write characters with excellence. Anyone can take a pen to paper, but few will give us an unforgettable experience through their work, and offer actors something to work with.

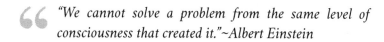 *"We cannot solve a problem from the same level of consciousness that created it."~Albert Einstein*

PATTERNS

> We are made of patterns. We are predictable even
> in our unpredictability.

Our patterns have varying shapes, colors, frequencies and intensities. No matter how unpredictable someone is, they become, eventually, predictable. They may be able to change pattern more often than the average person, mostly on surface level. It takes a little while longer to understand their cycle, because there are more patterns to go through. Still, we are all bound by repetition. Predictable people are consistent and use a limited amount of behavioural pattern. It is the difference between drawing a simple square verses drawing a mosaic. *Don't we call a boring person a square?*

EVERY SINGLE ORGANISM has a set of unique pattern, yet fits perfectly within the canvas of life. It is possible to alter our pattern. It is our responsibility to paint a more beautiful picture to better serve the collective mosaic. If you are contributing with a little square, you create a gap in the collective canvas. If you are oversharing with chaotic patterns that are tarnishing someone else's, you are destroying the canvas. Each one of us does make a difference to the whole, whether by negative or positive participation. We intuitively know we are connected, which is why we feel deeply offended when someone takes another person's life, as they create a gap in the collective. Homophobes get offended, because they feel vulnerable to being homosexual since someone else chose to be. We operate on a primitive level of consciousness through much of our instinctive reactions to someone else's choices. When we dig deep and understand our personal primal fears, we can finally bring into our consciousness, and rise to a higher consciousness, where pettiness turns to understanding of the self and others. This is one of the most important messages, because it is critical to your health, be it mental, emotional, physical, spiritual, or material.

If you watch closely, history does nothing but repeat itself. What we call chaos is just patterns we haven't yet recognized. What we call random is just patterns we can't yet decipher. What we can't understand we call nonsense. What we can't read we call gibberish. We need to sift through the patterns to see what needs dismantling and untangling. We can break the patterns, once awareness sets in. We need to clean up our own mess, and stop being lazy about fulfilling our purpose. Traumatic events create dark and tangled patterns within us. While we have to confront them, to heal them, we have to be careful with developing an addiction to the process. We have to put a deadline to it. The only way to create new patterns is by knowing when to stop staring at the existing one. Healing is a lifelong process. But it is up to you to unlock it and flush it out.

We can master our energy. We don't have to be
slaves to our history. Color yourself anew.

Visualize your existing pattern that needs altering. You can paint your patterns, using geometric shapes and colors dead center of a white paper. Use water colors. This is the existing pattern. Looking at it, you see that it is time to change it and release it. If you keep staring at your work of art there, it will dry up and cling to the paper evermore. But, if you bend the paper slightly from both ends, or hold it like a loose cone, then slowly poor water over it, it will drain from the bottom end and cause the pattern to fade as it flushes out. Then visualize new patterns and colors being created. As they increase, they will naturally wipe the old pattern off the paper. This is what our essence looks like. Forget your body temple. All we are is a pattern.

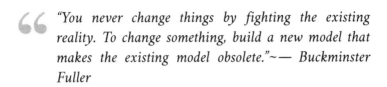 *"You never change things by fighting the existing reality. To change something, build a new model that makes the existing model obsolete."~— Buckminster Fuller*

SPIRALS

Life moves in Spirals. No matter how much I
   know about something, I always tell myself,
   pending further information.

We are not necessarily born with a clean slate due to hereditary influences. However, at one point in time, we began at ground zero. With every round of life stage, we learn a new lesson. At the second round, we may receive the same lesson more deeply. Every round makes us more insightful. We mustn't be arrogant when it comes to life lessons, because there is always deeper truths to be uncovered. We cannot possibly understand something to its end in one go. As is the case in schools, the higher our consciousness, the deeper the insight. If we do not get the lesson, we repeat it. If we do get it, we receive an advanced version of it. It goes on and on, until the projection is at its collective end.

"As above, so below."~The Emerald Tablet, The Hermetic Code

"Spiral upward into love & light"

THE SOUL

Our soul is boundless and filled with light. It is
love.

Everyone's soul is beautiful. When we see into someone's soul, we will be filled with boundless love and compassion. It reveals itself in moments of vulnerability. Our soul gets buried under the rubble and debris of traumatic experiences.

The severity of our trauma varies. In extreme cases, the soul escapes. We are called to unearth it and retrieve it. The beauty of the soul is that it never gets truly lost forever. It sometimes leaves to protect itself, until we offer it a safe haven once again. Let us do away with all things that are not ours to keep. Put

down the weight of your past. Heal your broken heart. Unify
your broken mind. Lose the names others called you by. Purge
all trauma. Dig deep, and don't stop until you have cleaned out
all the dust you gathered over the years. You are beautiful. You
are beautiful. Abandon the ugly ways, because you are
beautiful. Make space for your soul to come home.

> We can only lose what isn't ours. Anything that
> can be lost is never a loss. Anything that is ours,
> can never be taken away.

Soul Loss: Dark Night of the Soul

> When the soul escapes, we enter the dark night of
> the soul. But if it wasn't for the darkest hour,
> the soul would have no time to rest.

Have you ever looked at someone's eyes and found them
devoid of life? Psychopaths' eyes are mostly reported to be
empty. There is no trace of humanity in those eyes. Non-
psychopaths; however, can experience a different kind of
emptiness. We see it when we look in the mirror and fail to
recognize ourselves. This occurs in times of extreme sadness
and inner turmoil. Many of us lose sight of who we are when we
are in a painful time of our life. Your eyes that were once filled
with hope and joy are now lifeless. When we are unhappy or
drained, we feel a deep loss of our life force. When we are
surrounded by toxicity, and we get wounded, a piece of our soul
escapes our body temple to protect itself. With every wound,
physical or emotional, and with every trauma, and every
heartbreak, another piece escapes. The greater the toxicity, the
more lifeless we become. The good news is, there are ways to
retrieve the pieces of your soul. It does not have to be a
permanent condition. When we remove ourselves from the

environment that created the wounds, and set out to tend to them, clean them up, and heal, we become a safe space for the soul to return. The toxicity can be instigated by us just the same. In this case, you must alter the way you treat yourself and others. If you are the perpetrator, then a dramatic behavioural change is called for.

THINGS THAT CAUSE SOUL LOSS

- Any form of abuse, be it emotional, mental, sexual, physical, financial or spiritual.
- Traumatic events that have not been processed. It can range from prolonged childhood abuse, public humiliation to loss of a loved one through divorce or death.
- Committing crimes, going to war, and any engagement in high conflict situations.
- Prolonged substance abuse of any kind.
- Witnessing a crime or fatal accident.
- Suffering extreme poverty.
- Being diagnosed with a potentially fatal disease.
- Being victimized by a partner or a trusted person.
- Victims of kidnapping, human trafficking, and rape.
- Abusing others, bullying, being envious and engaging in malicious acts.

SYMPTOMS OF SOUL LOSS

- A marked emptiness in the eyes.
- Constant fatigue no matter how long you rested.
- Lack of focus and direction.
- Vertigo, and overall loss of balance.
- Irritability and violent outbursts.

- Low vibrational energy.
- Mental numbness.
- Perpetual emotional pain that leads to addictions.
- Inability to connect with others.

Dream yourself infinite. Leave yourself some
   breathing space.

SOUL RETRIEVAL

Call your soul back home.

Many of us have created a hostile environment for our soul. When we wage wars within our mind, and our body attacks itself, our souls get evicted. To retrieve it, we must cease fire. Gradually, the pieces will return, with one act of truce at a time. Love and fear cannot occupy the same space. When fear populates your mind, it clouds the soul 's loving light. Only when we let go of our darkness can we see clearly again. Make yourself a safe haven; invite the light back in.

1. Mind your thoughts. Get rid of negative self-talk. Talk to yourself the same way you would talk to your child or someone you love.

2. Refrain from alcohol, and chemicals. (I am not advocating against them. But they obstruct inner light.)

3. Remove all harmful people from your life.

4. Eat nurturing food.

5. Sleep well every night, preferably at the same hour.

6. Meditate every morning and every night.

7. Get rid of your addictions.

8. Go to therapy, seek trusted healers. Make use of Nature.

9. Forgive yourself for past mistakes, expectations, and missteps.

10. Forgive others by releasing resentments and anger. Do

not invite them back into your life, if they continue to be abusive.

11. Take good care of your overall health. Visit doctors when needed. Bring back your joy.

12. Revisit your goals and dreams, and make time for them each day.

13. Surround yourself with genuine people, who add value to your life.

14. Be mindful of what you watch, and listen to. Practice intentional entertainment.

15. Slow down. Refrain from judging yourself, and release judgments of others. Do not engage in gossip or chronic complaining. What you say affects your energy.

16. Stop blaming yourself, people, or circumstances. Raise the standards of your life and take responsibility.

17. Have integrity in everything you do. Write down all the characteristics of someone you admire, then set out to embody those characteristics in yourself.

18. Do not allow anyone to disrespect you. Have self-respect and healthy boundaries.

19. Do not behave in ways that do not represent and honor who you are. Take past lessons and make wiser choices.

20. Have a zero tolerance policy for anything that does not align with your higher self and new found, healthy lifestyle.

21. Learn to be receptive to love.

WOUNDED HEALERS

> I trust healers, who have been wounded, and
> respect the wounded, who become healers.

Some people let their wounds turn them cold; others use them to be of service. Those, who choose a path to healing themselves are courageous. We all heal a little when someone shares their story, and the lessons they gained through their journey. Academic guidance pales against that of experience.

I HAVE BEEN fortunate to find therapists, who merged their academic studies with their humanity, empathy, and receptivity. Therapists, who are genuinely capable of empathy, can be all the healing we need. After all, this what we are starved for. When therapists are grounded, and not biased, they become valuable anchors for us until we find our own. With their rich knowledge, and generosity of spirit, we feel safe and empowered.

AUTHENTIC SHAMANIC HEALERS dedicate themselves for our collective well-being. They hold space for us when we are unable to hold space for ourselves. Opening our heart space and healing our minds are valuable gifts for those willing to receive it. Setting out to turn your wounds into pearls of wisdom is a great gesture of self-love and respect. One of the ways to heal yourself is by helping someone else.

WHEN WE SHARE our experience with someone, we both feel less alone. Like all healers, we must make great sacrifices. But what we sacrifice will prove not to be a sacrifice at all. We will be sacrificing outdated beliefs, shedding old skin, and releasing emotions we no longer need. We have to sacrifice everything that has been weighing us down. We will sacrifice our emotional laziness and overall sluggishness. The rewards will be beyond your imagination, if only you are willing.

· · ·

Spiritual Bypassing

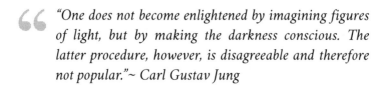 *"One does not become enlightened by imagining figures of light, but by making the darkness conscious. The latter procedure, however, is disagreeable and therefore not popular."~ Carl Gustav Jung*

A suppressed shadow turns itself into a tribe of inner demons, who will run your life. Artists are alchemists, who often feel comfortable with their darkness, and they use their work to channel them out into gold. An artist, who is not creating, or sharing their work, becomes ill. They know that shadows do not survive the light. No matter how scary the darkness may be for you, it needs to be exposed. New paths will brighten up for you. Sooner or later, everything that is in the dark shall come to the light. The process will happen with or without your help.

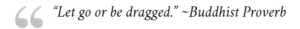 *"Let go or be dragged." ~Buddhist Proverb*

Toxic Healing

Enough, with all the healing; let us embrace the
perfect mess we are.

Sometimes, acceptance is all the healing we need. Using Meditation as a form of emotional suppression is dangerous. It is not always about calm music, closing your eyes, and saying OM. It is found just as well in moments of presence with a lover, in moments of heartbreak and despair, in humbling moments and joyful ones, in creativity and playfulness. I have found healing at rock bottom, and learned surrender during times life has brought me to my knees. I felt god as I was staring down the barrel of a gun. Healing is a messy, and destructive process.

Using healing techniques mustn't be an answer to a trend. It will make you sick when it's forced. Don't fall victim to a glorified healing method that may not be healthy for you. We are all unique, so what may be right for one, is not necessarily right for another. Meditation is an ancient practice and everyone does it, whether they know it or not. However, when it became trendy, many flocked to meditation centers without being properly guided. They pressured themselves into feeling better. It doesn't work this way. Mindless meditation suppresses the emotions further, and is dangerous to your mental health. We cannot breathe our way through anger, grief, and loss, without confronting them. Everything in existence needs acknowledgment before it resolves itself.

OVER THE PAST few years we witnessed a shocking rise in Ayahuasca tourism. This is a potent, spiritual plant. I believe in the powerful, healing properties of Ayahuasca and Nature in general. I have friends, who healed from cancer, auto-immune diseases and chronic depression. Ayahuasca saved me from suicidal thoughts. But no one is in a position to tell you what is good for you and what is not. Only you know what you need, what is right for you, and what is not right for you. Only you are responsible for your choices. Our journeys are as unique as our night dreams. There is a dark side to every path. False healers will keep you hooked on the healing loop. It becomes toxic when we become addicted to its cycle. There has to come a time when you move into acceptance and gratitude for the lessons, rather than playing the same tape in the same loop. Ask yourself what you are gaining by remaining victimized and stuck in your old stories?

. . .

Toxic Positivity

> There is a trampoline at the bottom of your abyss.
> What you push down will find its way out.

Turning a blind eye to what we must confront will never be a path to well-being. The positivity craze is just that... a craze. Emotions not validated create monsters within us. These monsters set up camp in your psyche, and keep growing, and having children, and when they have a big enough army, they will wreak havoc on your life. Don't let people tell you to stop expressing how you feel.

When we express our dark emotions to share and find resolutions, we get to heal. People will tell you how everything happens for a reason, and while that I believe to be true, it mustn't be used as a way to belittle someone's pain. Allow your loved ones to grieve. Don't let yourself or anyone keep you sick.

BEING EXCLUSIVELY POSITIVE IS MADNESS. People, harboring toxic positivity, are also some of the angriest people around. Shunning your shadow and the dark side of life leads to spiritual bypassing and is detrimental to your overall health. This can lead to psychosis. Still, we have to be responsible with whom we choose to share.

WHEN WE UNLOAD UNTO OTHERS, they may not be able to bear the weight of what we are sharing. We have to be responsible with what we bring into someone's space. Toxic positivity has broken many friendships. When we stop receiving each other whole, we are essentially asking our loved ones to suppress half of themselves. We pretend to be happy when we are not, and we stop sharing our truth with those closest to us. We avoid being called negative, dramatic and weak, so we put on a mask.

WHEN THE LAW of Attraction became a thing, it destroyed much of our relationships, and severely damaged the way we receive each other. It steered us into a delusion that all we had to do is say positive affirmations and all will be well.

EVER SINCE THAT law became common knowledge, I became increasingly frustrated with the fantastic expectations many had of themselves and others. It is irresponsible to promote falsehood by omission.

THE "LAW OF VIBRATION" is about self-responsibility. We emit the energy we want to attract. We must be responsible with the energy we bring into the world, and into each others' space. How radiant or dimmed we are affects how the world responds to us. You cannot use the law of attraction without adhering to all other laws of Nature, especially The Laws of Vibration and of Inspired Action.

WITHOUT TAKING THE NECESSARY ACTION, then there will be no desired result. Attraction does not happen, magically. The collective laws deserves their own book; the law of attraction, on its own, does not. Had there been a book that only addressed The Law of Vibration, we may have prevented many from becoming passive and delusional.

* * *

The 12 Laws Of The Universe

When we are not integrating all the laws, we become naturally fragmented. Going against the laws of Nature is the root cause of everything going against us. Flow with Nature. It is the only way to peace.

Here are the 12 Laws:
- The Law of Divine Oneness
- The Law of Vibration
- The Law of Correspondence
- The Law of Attraction
- The Law of Inspired Action
- The Law of Perpetual Transmutation of Energy
- The Law of Cause and Effect
- The Law of Compensation
- The Law of Relativity
- The Law of Polarity
- The Law of Rhythm
- The Law of Gender

> What good is the Law of Attraction, when you
> bypass the 11 others?

Receptive Mode

> We only receive what we think we are worthy of
> receiving.

We are always in receptive mode, but not always aware of what we are open to receive. When we are receptive to something, we may not be receptive to another.

To have and to keep what we are praying for, we must be able to receive it. If we lose our sense of self-worth, we create blockages. If our beliefs about ourselves are in sharp contrast to what we ask for, we create resistance. Sometimes false beliefs are passed down over generations, yet no matter how much we disagree with them, we often internalize them still.

Here are two common examples:

1. ON MONEY and Wealth
   False belief 1: "Money is the root of all evil".
   False belief 2: "Money doesn't buy happiness."
   False belief 3: "Money is my power."

MOST PEOPLE WANT to be rich, and most struggle with acquiring material wealth. You may have internalized the aforementioned beliefs, which created the resistance. Cognitive dissonance prevents you from being receptive to blessings. Even when you do receive it, you lose it at a stunning speed.

Think of all those, who won the grand Lottery and lost it within 6 months. Or, those, who went from rags to riches, only to lose it all through self-destruction. Subconsciously, they are sabotaging the blessing they are internally judging, or feel unworthy of.

THE FIRST BELIEF implies that all evil in the world is created by money. Evil is created by people. It can be due to greed, jealousy, or lust. But not all people, who have money are evil. Money is one of the main motivations for crime, but it can also be a means to create, build, donate, and serve.

· · ·

THE SECOND BELIEF is equally destructive, because it is quite common to see unhappy rich people, and happy poor people, but that does not mean that you do not need money in a materialistic world. You need money to take care of your health, medical bills, put food on the table, have running water and electricity, go on trips, buy clothes, take care of your family and your pets, feed your mind, and the list is endless.

BEING unfulfilled is a personal obstacle regardless of wealth. Material wealth is not enough to make you fulfilled. You have to do the inner work. But it certainly won't serve you to be poor, and unable to meet your basic survival needs either.

THE THIRD BELIEF that your power can be found in money may be true in this day and age, but it is not authentic power. Some people extract their power through material wealth, so to pay you, they believe they're giving their power away. They won't care that you can't afford food, let alone pay off your own debts. This impact you and everyone else relying on you. This is why some wealthy people fight you over insignificant amounts. To them, paying you is giving you some of their power, and they cannot afford to lose control over you. When power is extracted from the material, the person can easily feel disempowered whenever they have to part with some of it.

2. ON LOVE
    False belief 1: "I am unworthy of love."
    False belief 2: "All men cheat."
    False belief 3: "Unconditional love does not exist."
    False belief 4: "I will never find anyone to love me."

. . .

PEOPLE, who experienced childhood abandonment, internalize the belief that they are unworthy of love. They never learned how to love themselves, because no one loved them in their formative years. If they feel unworthy to such a degree that they deny it themselves, it will be more intensified when it's offered from others. Not knowing how to receive it, they may sabotage and resent it.

THE SECOND BELIEF is that all men cheat. So much is wrong with this statement. Generalizations obstruct truth. Why is it usually about men, anyway? Some people cheat, from both genders, and some don't. You have to be mindful of what you believe, because what you look for is what you will find. The end.

THE THIRD BELIEF IS AN OXYMORON. It implies that conditional love exists. There is no such thing as conditional love, because love, by its nature has no conditions. You can have conditional acceptance, attention, or respect, but not love.

THE FOURTH IS as true as you make it out to be. If you believe no one will ever love you, then you will not recognize it when it is offered. It can appear rather boring, because it is uncomfortably unfamiliar.

AS CLICHÉ AS IT IS, no one can offer you love unless you know how to accept it. If you are used to unloving relationships, you will not find those willing to offer love to be appealing. You will think no one would love you, when really, it is you who is rejecting the offering.

. . .

REPLACING RESISTANCE FOR RECEPTIVITY

1. Question your beliefs, and pin point the ones that are neither true, nor helping you.

2. Replace false and disempowering beliefs with empowering ones.

3. Instill your new beliefs through daily mantras until you change your subconscious tape.

4. Set clear intentions and be as specific as possible.

5. Do not share your visions with anyone. Many people may intentionally or unintentionally project their limitations on you. Protect your dreams at all cost.

* * *

KARMIC CONTRACTS

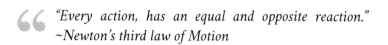 *"Every action, has an equal and opposite reaction."*
~Newton's third law of Motion

According to Eastern spiritual philosophy we have come into being after signing up for specific roles, and there were contracts involved. These contracts can be fulfilled or broken. Breaking a karmic contract, or karmic ties to someone, can be done with intentional meditation. If reincarnation is something you believe in, you'd understand that we have created a dynamic with others that may have begun in past lives.

If you have met someone in a past life, you'd both be paying for that karmic debt in this one, and it can carry on to the next. To end unfounded animosity, we need to break the toxic ties. Once we learn our karmic lessons, we no longer need to revisit them.

* * *

KARMA

What is your karma, and how can you exonerate
yourself from it?

Most people think karma is a debt you have to pay for what harm you have done to others, or the return for the good you have done to others. This is one aspect of it. It is an internal process just as much as it is external. Karma encompasses your actions, thoughts, and emotions. The energy you produce returns to you. We get punished by our negative emotions, and thoughts, and not necessarily because of them. Karma, is you in action. We get punished and rewarded in direct relation to what we feel and radiate. Our emotional reaction to an event creates a karmic current that renews and intensifies the emotions within us. We relive the experience in different forms and through different people.

AN EXAMPLE of how karma can work internally:
Habiba was betrayed by her mother, who abandoned her and neglected her needs as a child. Later in life, Habiba started to have relationship trouble. She had a hard time trusting others and developed a severe fear of abandonment. Her karma is caused by holding on, unknowingly, to resentment and anger towards her mother. It catches up with her through dysfunctional romantic relationships.

BECAUSE HABIBA WAS TRIGGERED by a toxic relationship that she recognized the resemblance between her current experience, and that of her past, she shifted her focus on the original offender, and took steps to forgive her mother. She no longer needed to exert tremendous effort to release herself from her man. His role was done.

Once Habiba goes through this deep process, her relationships begin to heal as a natural byproduct of that. She finds herself choosing partners with a healthy mindset, rather than being subconsciously pulled towards those, who will help her play out her old familiar narrative.

It takes a special mindset to notice one's patterns, and courage in facing one's roots, and act on the new awareness. The key is in your hands; no one else's. If we hold on to anger, our karma is more anger. When we release it, we are rewarded by the liberation from it.

> We fall in love with people, who resemble the
> parent we need to forgive most.

* * *

RELEASING KARMIC CORDS

KARMIC TIES ARE STRUNG within us through the emotions we feel about them. While we can be victimized by someone's action or inaction, we have the power to stop the karmic wheel in its tracks by not retaliating on others or on ourselves.

Reacting or responding to a karmic event is on you, while the action of the perpetrator is on them. Sometimes, what you perceive as bad may not be so.

Waiting for the other person's karma to go into effect will only darken yours. Everything has its purpose.

Even though I believe no one gets away with anything, good or bad, the act of waiting for a payoff prolongs karmic justice and we end up magnifying our emotions about it. So, creating positive karma and releasing negative ones make a massive difference in how the rest of our lives are shaped.

HOW TO RELEASE KARMIC CONTRACTS:

1. Ask what lessons have you gained from the experience.

2. Practice forgiveness.

3. Sit in a quiet space, and use your Active Imagination skills. In your mind's eye, see yourself in an empty room with two chairs facing each other.

Notice a pair of scissors in your hand. Sit on one of the chairs, and have the person you have a karmic tie with in the other chair. Then visualize a cord that is coming out of your heart space to theirs.

Tell them everything you want to tell them and the impact of their actions on you. When you're done, it's their turn to answer. Hear them out. You might find yourself putting words in their mouth. This is normal. Get quiet again, and intuitively, allow them to defend themselves.

Keep the conversation going until you have covered all aspects of it. Refrain from circular thinking. Be efficient and to the point.

When you can understand where they are coming from, you offer them forgiveness. Announce that you have received the lesson well.

Thank them and bless them. Take the scissors, and visualize yourself cutting the cord from your heart's end and then from their end. Tell them they are released, and bid them farewell. Picture them get up and leave the room.

YOU CAN DO this with as many people as you like. You can use it with a deceased person you have unfinished business with, and you can use it to ask for forgiveness just the same.

ANIMAL GUIDES

> An invocation: As I walk through this earth, I am
> open to receive the guidance of spirit, knowing
> my spirit animals are here to protect me from
> harm.

Every person is assigned an *Animal Totem* by birthright. This is the animal that guides and protects you throughout your life journey. Assigning an animal totem to a character intensifies its depth beautifully. It offers insights and clues as to how they act, move, and what their values are. Exploring their shadow side is equally important. Like humans, every animal has a light side and a dark side. Through their fears and instincts, we understand their motivations and vulnerabilities. Researching an animal helps you map out your set of character traits, beliefs, values and lessons. When you are receptive to animal guidance, you enjoy their wisdom that can be easily applied in your life. As for *Spirit Animals, they* are available to anyone at any time. Once you know your animal totem, or if you want to understand your spirit and power animals, it is always great to watch them on Animal Planet, and check for spirit animal websites. Shamanic teachings offer valuable information on this topic. Below is the breakdown:

1. *Animal Totem:* This is who you are in essence; it is your animal mirror. It watches over you and protects you. It is your advisor, if you are open to listen. This is the only animal that is constant.

My Animal Totem is **the Wolf.**

Wolf Quote: *"Be still and trust your intuition. Your song is heard."*

Some of the wolf's light qualities are: Grace, strength, insight, wisdom, loyalty and passion.

In his *shadow*, a wolf is: Fierce, territorial, intimidating, a loner, broken, and melancholic.

My guardian, the Wolf and I.

Native American Wolf Prayer

Spirit of the Wolf,
You who wanders the wild lands, You who stalks
in silent shadows, You who runs and leaps
between the moss-covered trees, lend me your
primal strength, and the wisdom of your
glowing eyes. Teach me to relentlessly track my
desires. And to stand in defense of those I love.
Show me the hidden paths and the moonlit
fields. Fierce Spirit, walk with me in my
solitude. Howl with me in my joy and guard me
as I move through this world.

2. *SPIRIT ANIMAL:* These are the animals that seem to appear to you everywhere at a certain time. Your soul knows it needs their guidance. They get your attention through dreams, meditations, and make an appearance everywhere you look. Pay attention to understand what message you need to receive about a current issue. Spirit animals keep appearing for you until you receive their message. You may have several spirit animals over a lifetime; they may act as a signal that you are about to go through a transition in your life or act as a warning to not go down a certain path.

THE TIMING

Spirit Animals don't necessarily appear briefly during setbacks. They may appear when a time for a personal metamorphosis is called for. When they disappear, it means that either their job is done, or they felt offended by your dismissal. If you are not receptive to them, they move on. They may return to you on more than one occasion with increased urgency. But if you continue to ignore them, they will eventually stop. Enabling behavior is not within their jurisdiction. They will move on before the issue at hand is resolved when ignored. Not paying attention, lack of appreciation, and dismissal are acts of disrespect. Remember to offer them gratitude and blessings when they visit.

> Divine timing and intervention truly work in
> beautiful ways when we are open to receive
> them.

ANIMAL SPIRIT GUIDES IN HUMAN FORM

Your spirit animal can be a human being. We are animals too. Have you every encountered a stranger, who came to your aid and then suddenly disappeared, never to be seen again?

Have you had a conversation at the most opportune moment that saved you from mental anguish? These are our human angels acting as guides.

HUMAN SPIRIT GUIDES make themselves known through:
1. Chance encounters.
2. An unexpected call from a friend in a moment of need.
3. A dream.

> It is truly a gift to have animal guides walk with you on the path. Let them guide you through your darkest hours and remain receptive to their *divine wisdom.*

Examples:

KANGAROO: During a 5-day intensive Ayahuasca Ceremony, we were given an option on the third day to drink the Daime as we take a long walk through the forest. Being the couch potato that I am, I decided to welcome something new. I am here to change my patterns after all. My father had been diseased a year and 40 days prior. He appeared during the entire ceremony, and walked beside me that day. On our walk, deep in conversation, I heard the trees whisper. I looked to my right, and a Kangaroo was hopping away in the heart of a Dutch forest. Little did I know, Kangaroos are not to be found in the Netherlands. This was an animal spirit, here to tell me,

"DON'T LOOK BACK. It is time to move forward towards your future."

* * *

SNAKE: Snakes appeared to me in two instances; one as a warning, and the other for healing. Many kinds of snakes are venomous, which is why they became the symbol for healing and a common logo for pharmacies. Poison has often been used as medicine. As an ancient adage goes, "The poison that kills becomes the elixir of life when used by the wise." Snakes are revered in shamanic medicine just the same, as they often make an appearance during inner visions and journeys of spiritual ceremonies.

> "It is time to take your bitter medicine, because it
> is time to let go." The snake said.

My first encounter with snakes was during an Ayahuasca ceremony, when I was going through a process of a specific traumatic event in my past. That event had to do with my late father's wife. I had a strong intuition that she murdered him, and as a result of that, along with all the pain she has caused, I harbored deep seated anger and grief. This was the same ceremony I mentioned earlier, and so, my father's spirit was with me.

MOTHER AYAHUASCA IS a female mother figure that we often see in our visions. This particular day was quite intense. It took 12 hours of processing emotional and physical hell. I learned that we get punished by our own emotions and my task was to release my anger and grief. Emotions turned into snakes, twisting around inside, and my hair turned into a Medusa style. Purging was intense, and when I looked into my bucket, it was filled with all the snakes I had to purge, so I can be released from the toxic bond I had with this woman. When the ceremony was finally over, I could barely maintain my balance. I asked others how crazy they think it was to purge snakes? They laughed, because the snakes we encounter in a vision do not manifest in the 3D. Many see them independently, but we cannot share the same vision. After this ceremony, I have felt such deep gratitude I have never felt before, and understood what forgiveness truly means. We absolutely must release toxic emotions for our own sake.

> What a miracle it is that we can stand on our two
> feet, carrying all this emotional baggage!

The Second occasion snakes kept coming to me was at a time when I was dating a psychopath. Naturally, it was a deeply traumatic experience. He was charming, manipulative, and has a formidable talent to drive anyone completely insane. Now and then, I would wake up in tears due to a nightmare about a cobra. Every time I get this nightmare, it is doing the same thing… trying to kill me. It looked viciously angry and malicious. In the dreams, I always knew the snake was him. Dreams work in mysterious ways, and general interpretations don't work unless it is put into context. Make sure to use your intuition to get your personalized message. This psychopath was, both, a venomous and a healing snake. Venomous because the man was toxic in every way, and healing, because he was the catalyst that I discovered a wound I didn't know I had. Once I came to this realization, I slowly began to learn applying this lesson. Once the lesson was received and applied, I wrote him a letter of gratitude, and got him out of my life. Healing ourselves by turning poison into medicine is imperative.

* * *

I HAVE BEEN BLESSED with many human angels along the path. Some were strangers, and some were old friends. These are the ones that helped me regain my faith in humanity.

A stranger saved me from being stranded at an airport after I was subjected to a crime by someone I knew. An old friend, I haven't been in contact with, extended help, because he answered a vision of me that told him to reach out. An old man offered me wisdom that dried my tears, and many have stood by me, when I least expected it. I am forever grateful.

3. *Power Animal:* This is the animal you intentionally invoke through meditation, incantations, and so on, in a time of need. You choose them based on your need of a particular power. They can be animals or people. The specific friend you turn to for guidance will vary based on the nature of the guidance you need. Who we choose is determined by their support capacity in a particular situation. The one you call in an emergency may be different from the friend you call after a breakup. They do not always have to be someone familiar. Many times I would call upon the energy of a stranger that I admire, when I need help with grounding, confidence, or peace within. Many inspire us to defy our fears, motivate us to be better, and help us remember our inherent worth.

Shadow Animals

Our Shadow Animal Spirit represents the darker side of our personality. Using your shadow animal offers deeper insight into your behaviour in times of darkness. When actors approach a role, it serves them well to grasp their Shadow Animal, and not just settle for its light side. This applies to characters that are mostly good or heroic. Considering you already settled on your Animal Totem, separate its good qualities from its negative qualities.

Taking the Wolf as an example, in its power and light, the

Wolf is a leader, a great communicator, in tune with his song, and a ferocious protecter of his pack and territory. In his shadow, he can be vicious when cornered, a loner, melancholic, and broken. Observing your Animal Totem closely will help you with embodying it, and with understanding yourself better.

A tip: Your instinct is the most reliable source to know what your animal totem is. But if you're not in tune with your intuition yet, then here's another exercise:

Write down your most significant characteristic. Then google one at a time by asking, which animals are, for example, nocturnal? Which animals are psychopathic? Which animals are the most joyful or loyal? You will always get a long list of animals that meet one characteristic, but as you go through them, the list will keep narrowing down the results.

KNOWING YOUR ANIMAL TOTEM, and Spirit Guides:

The key word is "knowing". Tap into your inner knowing, and you will intuitively have the answer. Here are a few prompting questions for Animal Totems:

1. WHEN I look at my characteristics, which animal do I resemble the most?

2. Which animal have I always sensed a deep connection with, and felt is always protecting me spiritually?

3. Which animal do I feel a deep sense of inexplicable familiarity with?

YOU DON'T HAVE to answer. Just ask these questions before bed or during meditation, and let the answers come to you.

. . .

HELPFUL TIPS:

1. STRENGTHEN your intuition through daily meditation.

2. In a meditative state, think of the animal guide you need. You can say, I am open to receive guidance from my spirit animals.

3. Avoid alcohol and drug consumption in a time of turmoil. Meditate before bed and ask to be guided.

4. Become aware of your surroundings. They make appearances in the oddest of places. They can appear in a painting, on social media, an old birthday card, etc.

5. They may make their presence known through other senses. You may hear them, as you do a hummingbird, an owl, or a wolf howling, especially if they do not inhabit your area. You may smell them, feel a taste in your mouth that triggers a memory of a certain animal, plant, or possibly a human. (To each their own, I'm not here to judge).

ANIMAL SOUNDS ARE TREMENDOUSLY HEALING. The purring of a cat on your tummy emits healing vibrations as it helps circulate and renew your energy, and release sadness. A wolf's howl is a reminder of your inner power demonstrated with beauty, melancholy and inspires effective communication. A hummingbird in the Egyptian culture offers hope that your prayers and wishes are being heard and answered.

May you walk safely upon the earth, knowing your
guides are protecting you.

* * *

ALIENS & EXTRATERRESTRIAL BEINGS

> We cannot conceive of that which does not exist. It
> cannot make its way into our consciousness.
> Extra-terrestrial intelligence has made its
> presence known.

It is no coincidence that the way movies depict aliens are a carbon copy of those, who enter our psychedelic visions. People have reported identical visions. Every psychedelic plant brings its unique beings that communicate to us. Even when films depicted them in a primitive way, they weren't far off. The language they speak in is melodic. They are in complete flow with their roles in the Universe. Debates are ongoing as to how Ancient Egyptians built the pyramids, and many have claimed they were built by aliens. I believe, when we set ourselves in an expanded consciousness state, and our senses are heightened, that we become attuned to their higher vibrations; we receive their powers. Equally, beings of the underworld; namely, those vibrating at low frequencies, make their appearance in dreams and depictions of demonic possessions. From Out of Body experiences to Sleep Paralysis, we encounter all forms of extraterrestrial life. If you want to encounter one, you have to match your vibrational frequency to it. People, suffering from Schizophrenia, report visions through their paintings. Sometimes I wonder if they are not suffering at all, and enjoying an overactivity of DMT in their brain that results in extrasensory abilities. All I know is what I have encountered, and how our frequency can attune us to incredible worlds.

* * *

CHAPTER 4
THE PSYCHOLOGY REALM

STAGES OF CONSCIOUSNESS

Some believe that we use 10% of our brain power, which, in my opinion, is false. Our behaviour is mostly driven by our subconscious mind, which occupies 88-90%. We do use 100% of our minds. There is a confusion between the mind and the brain. The former is an intangible entity that hosts our thoughts, awareness and memory; the latter is an organ. It is impossible to measure it in general terms. It varies from person to person.

THE CONSCIOUS MIND

Everything we are aware of is in the conscious mind. It is responsible for 10-12% of our behaviour. I am not sure if this is measurable, because the amount of stored data we retrieve from our subconscious mind and into our conscious mind varies from person to person. Some people spend their lives bringing their suppressed memories and deep-seated wounds into their conscious mind, to release it, while others exert effort to keep their shadow dormant.

One of the most frustrating transitions in my life was when I became aware of my unconscious behaviour and what was triggering it. Once aware, I would notice when my old impulses would resurface, and I feel the urge to act in my old ways, but due to my awareness, I was no longer able to allow myself to succumb to it. I was calling myself out on my own bullshit. After a while, the impulses lessened. They can resurface when we are cornered or pressured, but it becomes far in-between, with much less intensity, and you snap out of it a lot faster.

THE SUBCONSCIOUS MIND

Most people are dominated by their subconscious mind. The subconscious doesn't discern good from bad, or right from wrong. All it knows is, *"What I know is good, and what I don't know is bad". It is primitive, and potentially dangerous.* For example, a child that was physically abused, grows to believe that abuse equals love, and that he/she deserves the punishment. Even though when they grow up to intellectually understand that abuse is not acceptable, they find it hard to separate it from love, and go on to commit to abusers, or avoid intimacy altogether. Most of us are running on auto-pilot. The more we shed light on what is embedded in our subconscious and bring it into awareness, our behaviour becomes less automatic, and more mindful. We will need time to process the information, so we can genuinely stop it from having a hold on us. We know the process is complete, when we are no longer reacting or sinking into survival mode.

THE CRITICAL MIND

The critical mind is the dividing line between our conscious and subconscious minds. It forms gradually later in life, and enables us to develop discernment skills. It protects us from being suggestible, and gullible. The danger of not exercising critical thinking is that it weakens that filter. This makes us susceptible and vulnerable to manipulation and mind control. This is why subliminal messages, fear induced tactics, repetitions, and doctrines work so well.

WE ARE NOT RATIONAL BEINGS.

Corporations know that it is not about the product, but our emotions about it that turn us into addicts. Some products leave us obsessed. We go to great lengths to have it, even if we don't need it. Before the critical mind is developed, everything goes straight into our subconscious. This is the time we are most vulnerable to trauma. The saddest thing is when toddlers and young children are exposed to traumatic events, they become primed for future trauma. Everything is recorded in their subconscious, and it takes decades, if not more, to recover from it.

Those with healthy childhood, trauma can break through their critical mind in adulthood, depending on how severe it is. Its gravity can penetrate the mental barrier. Some have barriers stronger than others. It can be a trauma in and of itself to be subjected to hardships after decades of a sheltered life. Children, whose parents were enmeshed, kept them in a protective bubble, did not do their children a service. They prevented them from being well-prepared for life's inevitable setbacks. They crack at the first minor challenge.

A healthy critical mind is open to receive foreign information, and scrutinizes it, before taking it in. Having a weak barrier, we become easily victimized. A rigid barrier prevents growth, tolerance, understanding, and the ability to enjoy new experiences. It keeps us imprisoned by our own ideas, which can lead to fanaticism. When we are unable to accept new information, our mind becomes fragile, and our brain cells die.

THE ENLIGHTENED MIND/THE NO MIND

> *"You are not your thoughts."~Chuck Palahniuk, Fight Club*

I believe the enlightened mind is one that discerns between the observer self, and the observed; the greater the distance, the more enlightened the mind. Whenever I notice that I'm taken in too far into a thought, I stop, and visualize myself stepping away from it. This is how we regain objectivity. It is to remind myself to refrain from identifying with my ego projections, especially when it gets too crazy. Those moments of an enlightened state feel like absolute bliss. Practiced consistently, we will be able to lead with it. I don't know if anyone is able to live in that state fully, all the time. We hear stories of people, with a perpetual, quiet grace and peace. I do know, that it certainly becomes more and more accessible once you know how. But those, who claim to have killed their ego altogether are those, most likely, fully consumed by it. We cannot see what we become.

THE EGO

In our ego, we are walking, talking wounds.

It's easy to be trapped by our ego, because we have been conditioned early on to identify with it. The ego is a masterful trickster. It outsmarts me more than I would like to admit. Some people will ridicule you for having an ego, as if they don't. It tricks us into believing that we managed to defeat it. It takes the most massive ego to proclaim such a fantastic feat. We can; however, keep it at bay, and savor in the moments of its mini-deaths before it resurrects once again. Accepting it as part of our current reality can certainly help us see it for what it is.

We can quiet it down through grounding and awareness when we see it coming.

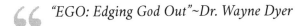 *"EGO: Edging God Out"~Dr. Wayne Dyer*

There are many misconceptions about the ego. The most common is associating it with an inflated sense of self. It can just as much manifest itself as a deflated sense of self. Playing small, and being a victim, is an equally present ego. It is a master manipulator; a shape shifter. It takes on many energies and forms, both familiar and unfamiliar. Throughout our lives, we uncover bits and pieces of the ego's magic tricks. We can observe it in ourselves and others. Recognizing it in others can help us understand how much we can hide it from ourselves. We can use what we recognize in others as an insightful blueprint for our ego and its behavioral patterns just the same.

> When we know the tricks, the magician is
> rendered powerless.

While we can't possibly know all of the tricks, we can take away the power of the ones we do know. Here are some masks our ego can appear in:

- Victimhood
- Arrogance
- Avoidance
- Narrow-mindedness
- Tyranny
- Depression
- Addiction

- Procrastination
- Judgment
- Maliciousness
- Passive-Aggression

The ego is our Shadow. I don't believe in the healthy ego concept. It is a deviation from soul. However, it does serve a purpose. It is because of these deviations that we learn how to return home. The positive aspects that stem from ego depend on whether we learn from it or not.

Knowledge is not power, unless we apply it.

In any event, being aware of it is all we could set out to do, to create change. Our job is to put our soul in the driver's seat. The ego is a dangerous driver. Put it in the backseat, in a baby carriage, and fasten the seat belt. Waging war against it is still ego. Acceptance and designation is key to quieting anything down, and minimizing its damage.

Tread carefully with your ego; it may run over
your soul.

WAYS TO TAME the ego

- Meditation
- Plant/Psychedelic Medicine
- Shadow Work
- Feedback from Friends
- Therapy/Hypnotherapy
- Connecting with animals
- Connecting with Nature

- Playfulness and Creativity
- Loving Partnerships

Things that bring our ego to its knees

- Tragedies
- Loss of a child
- Loss of a loved one
- Public Humiliation
- Material Loss
- Spousal Cheating
- Falling in Love
- Addiction
- Toxic People
- Abusive Relationships
- Victimization by Crime

DREAM STATES

In our dream states, we have an opportunity to connect with our soul. Our thoughts are silent, and we can download spiritual messages. Of course, we are vulnerable to nightmares too, but I am equally grateful for those. Nightmares let us know what we need to tend to in our lives; be it anxiety, a bad decision, or a certain fear we need to confront.

OUT OF BODY EXPERIENCES/ASTRAL PROJECTION

There are many methods out there to experience Astral Projection. My experience with it was not intentional, at first. It started early in life. Being able to see yourself as spirit, meeting with your angel guides is incredibly magical. There is a sense of liberation when you are no longer in the physical realm. The reason for this is because our egos don't join us there, and we are no longer imprisoned inside our body temple. It is a true lightness of being.

SURVIVAL MODE

People are most dangerous on survival mode.

Survival mode is being in a perpetual state of fear, even in the absence of a real and immediate threat. In this state, adrenalin, the stress hormone, peaks. *There are four types of fear responses:*

1. FIGHT 2. FLIGHT 3. FREEZE 4. PLEASE (FAWN)

IN A CONFLICT SITUATION, some people tend to go straight to *Fight*, while others respond with Flight. Freeze is quite common as well. Fawn is usually observed when the situation is prolonged such as in domestic violence.

We can, of course, respond differently based on the situation. The same person, who instigates bar fights may flee, freeze, or fawn, when confronted by his wife at home.

With a continuous threat of danger in war zones, or areas with a high crime rate, people's adrenalin will be highly active. This stress hormone is meant to be temporarily released to help save us from danger. But when it becomes a daily occurrence, we suffer PTSD and C-PTSD, which we delve deeper into in the next chapter.

* * *

FIGHT

When we are bombarded with code reds of impending danger, and due to overwhelming anxiety triggers we are exposed to in these times, we don't know what to do with all this anxiety, so we fight each other. The daily economical worries, relationship heartbreak, and betrayals, push many of us into addictions. Substance abuse, not only suppresses our emotions, but is fatal when combined with the stress hormones being released in our system such as adrenalin, oxytocin, and dopamine. It is a recipe for disaster. When we lose control over the situation, the only outlet we find is projecting anger and violence at random people. We cannot be reasoned with on fight mode.

FLIGHT

This response is positive when it prompts us to run from something that's about to eat us. It is not cowardly to run from someone threatening your life, but it is cowardly when we evade our responsibilities. Passive-aggressive behavior seems to have reached an all time high. Some people perceive heart-to heart-conversation to be equivalent to a gun pointed to their head.

Acts of cowardice are the most damaging. As mentioned earlier, without courage, we cannot possess any other virtue. A coward is far worse than a confrontational partner, because they fail to resolve anything, and refuse to be held accountable. If someone runs from their partner to avoid a conversation about a minor setback, then they cannot be trusted with real challenges either. In work environments, we have to deal with broken promises and serious financial setbacks thanks to flight mode.

. . .

FREEZE

When we are not able to comprehend and digest what is happening to us, we freeze. A helpless child is being bullied and harassed, and is unable to stand up for himself. The child knows no one will come to his aid. He figures that freezing is his only option. Later in life, he may develop a tendency to freeze in the face of emergencies and any form of confrontation.

Surely, he may rage at times, but the bigger the emergency, the more likely he is to freeze. He gets re-traumatized, even by something a lot less severe than the initial trauma. Due to the shame he internalized as a child, he sinks back into shame when he feels helpless. Unable to express himself as a grown man, who may be otherwise strong, chips away at his self-esteem. He feels weak. People, who have been physically abused, and reprimanded heavily for every perceived mistake, may freeze when they think they're in trouble. Have you ever noticed when you jokingly reprimanded your friend, and they become wide eyed, their ears turn red, and are not easily relieved once they realize it was only a joke? Children who were sexually abused often grow into freeze mode when someone makes unwanted advances towards them. They were conditioned that freezing is the only way for it to be over. Freezing can be traced back to living in the wild when humans and animals have to freeze to repel a predator. Playing dead can act as a saving grace.

4. FAWN: THE PLEASE RESPONSE

This survival mechanism is when a victim tunes in to her abuser and then adjusts her behavior to avoid triggering a violent outburst. It is not the same as empathy. Whereas empathy is done voluntarily, fawning is done out of necessity and with anxiety. Empathy is motivated by love; fawning is motivated by fear. The victim begins to identify with her abuser's identity, and emotions while misidentifying with her own. Now that she's fully attuned, she focuses on keeping her abuser happy, regardless of her own needs, goals, feelings, and general well-being. Fawning is an act of self-sacrifice and a moral self-mutilation. For this reason, it is the most draining and most painful survival mechanism. The most dangerous aspect of this response is that it keeps victims in an abusive relationship a lot longer, if not for life.

ADRENAL FATIGUE

Although there is no scientific acknowledgment to adrenal fatigue, it is a condition that creates extreme physical exhaustion caused by an overwhelming rush of adrenaline in our bodies. I trust it will make it into medical books soon. Many victims of abuse report adrenal fatigue. When your daily life is filled with anxiety, fear, intermittent reinforcement, and swings dramatically from one emotion to the next, you feel spent. The amount of natural chemicals that get released, or significantly drop at someone else's will, would make the best of us ill.

SOME SYMPTOMS OF ADRENAL FATIGUE:

- Constant fatigue, even if you slept well.
- Lack of focus, and anxiety-ridden.
- Vertigo.
- Derealisation.
- Low blood pressure.
- Depression.
- Emotional emptiness and lifelessness.
- Mentally drained.
- Loss of focus.
- Trauma-induced memory loss.

As you get emotionally stronger... as you fortify
your mind... the fear will fortify itself... it
mutates to match your newfound strength.
Don't let it discourage you. Eventually, fear will
give up, if you don't.

* * *

THE SHADOW SELF

The darkness of the moon gets illuminated. It
teases us with its cycles. It is beautiful in its
mystery, but magnificent when fully seen.
People are the same way.

Having it all is possible, if you are willing to accept both
sides of yourself; the light and the dark. One cannot embrace
half of life, while rejecting the other. By doing so, you get the
best of neither. All that is good for us has to include accepting
our darkness. Acceptance means we are willing to embrace it
without judgment, so we can have peace.

Whatever you ignore, magnifies. What you
embrace, fades.

CORE WOUNDS

Denial leads to neglect; neglect leads to regret.

Not all core wounds are caused by direct or deliberate abuse.
None of us can be prepared enough to raise children.
Psychology is a relatively newly accepted science. The older
generation considered it necessary for those deemed psychotic;
some thought it's a pseudo-science. It was a source of shame to

admit to needing psychiatric help. The way they raised children was often unknowingly abusive. Denial is a go-to state, whenever we are confronted with an uncomfortable truth, and that includes our emotional suffering. Whether your parent ordered you to smile when you needed to grieve, or accused you angrily of being too sensitive when you cried, you were essentially pushed to deny yourself the right to feel, and conditioned to hide your pain. The price we have to pay for denial is high. It takes a toll on our mental and physical health, while it chips away at our most important connections, including the one with our parents. Denial to any form of suffering will aggrandize it. One of the most damaging forms of emotional invalidation is when it is combined with being shamed. When my dog was sick, I sunk into denial despite the repeated comments that he didn't look well. The thought of losing him was too painful, and for a moment, it was easier to pretend he is ok. Luckily, it didn't last, and medical attention was sought. Children, who report being assaulted are often met with their parents' denial. This leaves the child feeling shamed, discredited, and felling more unsafe than they already did. We, inadvertently created a world that is hostile towards victims, which further emboldened molesters, rapists, and every day bullies. The deeper the oppression we experience the more violent the retaliation and opposition. Newton's third law of motion warns of having to be mindful with what we do or fail to do. Much of what used to be acceptable behaviour is now punishable by law, be it law of man or law of Nature.

HERE ARE SOME CORE WOUNDS, and their internalized messages:
REJECTION/SHUNNING/SCAPEGOATING: I have to hide who I am. I am shameful and a bad person. I must appear perfect to avoid rejection. I should try to belong. I will oblige others.

. . .

ABANDONMENT: I am unworthy of love. I am invisible. I am not enough. I will always be alone. If I don't cling, they will leave. If I leave first, then they can't abandon me.

BETRAYAL: I am alone. I am unsafe. I lost hope and trust. I am scared. I am unworthy of loyalty.

PHYSICAL/SEXUAL/MENTAL/EMOTIONAL ABUSE: I don't deserve happiness. I am doomed. It's my fault. I deserve it. The world is not safe. No one is there to protect me. People will judge me, if they find out. I am an object to be used and discarded.

Rewrite your inner dialogue.

THE MOTHER WOUND

Mothers are sacred land.

Our mother is our blueprint to what a woman is, and what love looks and feels like. From her, we get our sense of self. The role of mother sets the stage for our future attachment style, and how we carry ourselves in the world. She is our first attachment. She is our lifeline. While we are still in her womb, we are marinating in her physical, as well as her emotional being. Birth in itself is a form of trauma. It is a painful rite of passage. We are pushed into a foreign environment that feels unsafe, because it is unfamiliar. Babies need to be coddled and enveloped to feel safe. It is the closest they feel to the warmth of the womb.

Since babies can't see themselves, they get their sense of self through the mother. Bit by bit, we begin to explore ourselves. We raise our hands and feet in awe, still unaware they belong to us. Babies think that what they can see exists, and what they can't see, does not exist. This is why babies cry when their mother steps out of their line of vision, even for a second. They did not yet develop object constancy, which is the understanding that just because someone is gone, does not mean they don't exist, or that they will never return.

When we have a healthy relationship with our mothers, we develop a healthy object constancy. But what if a mother abandons her children? And how do you think motherless children feel when society shames them into showing respect, if their own betrayed their trust? Having children does not automatically make someone a mother.

> Not every woman who gives birth becomes a
> mother. Some mothers never birthed a child.

Society puts mothers on a pedestal so high that she is untouchable. Often, mothers are idealized to a degree beyond humanity's reach. The expected standards of her are easy not to reach. We all suffer from a mother wound in varying degrees. Having a mother wound is the deepest one there is, yet we are still creating an environment that doesn't acknowledge it, let alone heal it.

> When a mother is narcissistic, enmeshed, and self-
> absorbed, she treats her children as extensions
> of herself. They learn that love has to be
> earned, and trust must be blindly given, but
> never received.

Many females suffer from severe feelings of worthlessness, no matter how beautiful, intelligent, and successful they are. They repeat the pattern in their friendships and relationships which further confirms their belief that the world is cold and unsafe. The world echoes back to us what we believe about it, which confirms to them that they are unworthy of love. Yet, because their idea of safety is tied with danger, they continue to gravitate towards dangerous partners. They go on to find ways to earn the right to be loved by giving their values away, and continue to trust despite the overwhelming evidence that the other person is not worthy of it. When a mother is unavailable, physically or emotionally, all of our other relationships suffer, especially the one with ourselves. Severe abandoned fears land us in dangerous situations, all in the name of being accepted. We think, *if my mother doesn't love us then we must be unlovable.* We become suspicious of anyone showing us love, and often choose relationships that will mirror the one we had with our mother. We choose unavailable partners. It is less painful for us to believe we are unworthy of love than to admit to ourselves that our mother was an unloving woman. We spend our lives believing we deserve punishment, unhappiness and rejection. This wound is layered and complex, and I am designating another book for it. It cannot be resolved in a chapter. Motherhood has become a role that society held against us. The mother is blamed for anything wrong with the children. Women were pressured to stay at home. But when women realized they have the right to work and follow their dreams, they were shamed for it for a long time. When shaming women didn't stop them, the feminist movement was birthed, by men. This led many women to further abandon their innate feminine powers. The idea of women working shouldn't have been something we had to get permission for.

The reason I am not a feminist is because I believe it hurt us more than we already were. It created an energy of hostility between men and women, when we need to embrace each other. Feminine energy is the birthplace of creativity, authentic power, all nurturing, and emotionally intelligent. A working woman doesn't have to mean we acquire masculine qualities, and suppressing our feminine energy. Sacred femininity needs to be retrieved so we can let it lead our professional and personal lives. But when we go into fight mode, we only feed opposition. Embracing our feminine energy in all its glory is more powerful than tapping into the false power of bravado and aggression.

EVERY LIVING BEING HAS the right and freedom to do as they please as long as they do not cause harm. We must refuse to get permission for something that is ours by birthright. When we fight for our rights, are we not essentially giving power to those we fight with?

> That which ends with 'ist' is hostile. It promotes apartheid and opposition.

THE FATHER WOUND

> Fathers are the spine that holds it all together.

Fathers demonstrate how a man behaves. They set the standards for their daughters' future relationship with men in a platonic context, and the standard their sons need to expect from themselves. It is expected for a father to provide and instill order, but almost expected not to be available, physically and certainly not emotionally. When feminism took effect, some fathers took it as an opportunity to abandon their obligations altogether. The father wound; however, is not as deep as that of the mother, but not any less critical to address. Fatherless sons and daughters often lack a sense of direction, or sense of safety. A father's absence or enmeshment creates permanent scars. We need our fathers to give us strength as we move through the world, knowing he has our back. Without that, we feel broken, and struggle to find our worth and value. When fathers are not present, and fail to support their children, not just financially, but as a source of security in general, children turn into insecure adults. The pressure on men to provide, and set an example of manhood is truly great. In an unstable economy, and a world that pushes men to disconnect from their emotions and concerns, while constantly being badgered with accusations of inadequacy, many fathers feel incapacitated and scared. They believe they are not fit to be husbands and fathers. When women forget how much men suppress, they become relentless with demands and blame. Men are rarely offered appreciation and gratitude for what they do. It is often a thankless role. They have limited options to lessen their pain; they either become workaholics just to stay away from home, cheat, become violent, or leave without a trace.

Some men have, sadly, become spineless. They cannot protect others, if they lost sight of the true meaning of masculinity. Divine Masculinity has gone through a demise as a byproduct of suppressing, and destroying the Sacred Feminine.

Manhood has become equivalent to evading responsibility, abuse, manipulation, and aggression. Men find it cool to have many romantic interests, and even cooler to overpower other men. A true masculine is one, who protects others, including from himself. Equating muscles with power is like equating botox to beauty.

If men reject the guidance and healing energy of their feminine counterpart, they become as sick as many have become today. If it is a generation of men raised by oppressed women, who do we hold accountable? The attack on feminine energy has pushed many women into complicity. There has been a collective case of Stockholm Syndrome, where women have become violent against each other in defense of the very group that oppressed them in the first place.

Each gender has its battles, and instead of working together and holding space for each other, we project our internal battles onto each other.

THE CHILDREN, in turn, internalize this dynamic, and turn into victims and villains. It is now imperative to merge both energies within us, if we were to save this race from complete destruction. We must make a conscious choice to say, *"This cycle ends with us."*

THE MOST POWERFUL talk about the father wound took place on OWN led by Oprah Winfrey and Iyanla Vanzant. I highly recommend watching both parts; Fatherless Sons, and Daddyless Daughters.

ATTACHMENT STYLES

OUR ATTACHMENT STYLES can be healed. Here are the four types of attachment styles based on early attachment patterns:

1. Secure upbringing creates a secure attachment style.

2. Avoidant leads to dismissive attachment style.

3. Anxious/Ambivalent leads to pre-occupied attachment style.

4. Disorganized leads to fearful/avoidant attachment style.

NOTE: What is your attachment style, and who are you attracting? With practical healing, we can shift our styles.

* * *

Other Childhood Wounds

- Physical abuse by a parent or a sibling.
- Neglect, with no consistent adult supervision
- Child molestation.
- Scapegoating by the family, being exposed to excessive criticism, sarcastic jokes and overall bullying.
- Children who are expected to be perfect to earn their parents' approval.
- Spoiling children by permissiveness.
- Using children as pawns in the power struggle between the parents.
- Treating children as extensions of yourself.
- Smothering, and isolating.
- Fulfilling one's emotional needs through the child.
- Assigning the child adult responsibilities that takes away their childhood too soon.

* * *

Defining our Shadow

> "The shadow is ninety percent pure gold." ~Carl Gustav Jung

Our Shadow Self is what we keep hidden from others, and more often than not, from ourselves. The shadow is the part of us that is wounded, and suppressed. The more we suppress it, the more intensely it demands our attention, and eventually, retaliates. Most people try to keep their shadow at bay, because it causes them deep shame and fear. They hide it from others in fear of being rejected, judged, and abandoned. What we fear, we demonize and destroy. We project it unto others in the ugliest of ways. This is why free spirits often attract unjustified haters. Haters do not like to be reminded of their shadow, or because they falsely believe they don't have light of their own. Due to lack of inner acceptance, others find it ugly just the same. When we embrace it; however, and acknowledge it, others begin to embrace it too. Within this space of empathy, the shadow disappears.

* * *

How the shadow controls you:

> If you don't deal with your issues, your issues will
> deal with you.

The shadow operates in full power without your help. It runs your life when you don't take charge of it. You think you're in control by dismissing it, bur this only gives it more control over you. The danger lies in being at war without know it.

Here are some signs you are controlled by your shadow:

- Bursting into uncontrollable tears that bring you to your knees.
- Going into fits of uncontrollable rage that is not appropriate for the situation.
- Refusing to communicate your needs with clarity; engaging in passive-aggressive behaviors, including stonewalling, the silent treatment, evasiveness, and indirect sabotage.
- Numbing by indulging in substances, including excessive drinking, impulsive shopping, binge watching TV, social media, partying too much,

promiscuity, eating disorders (overeating, not eating
enough, bulimia and anorexia)

- Judgment, prejudice, jealousy, envy, maliciousness,
  greed
- Committing crimes.
- Being suicidal or having suicidal ideations; self-
  destructiveness, self-sabotage.
- Clinginess, toxic attachment, detachment,
  indifference, depression and mania.
- Excessive nightmares.
- Compassion Fatigue.
- Self-deprecation/degradation.
- Playing small, dimming your light, people pleasing.
- Abusive and toxic relationships/friendships.
- Carrying shame and being vulnerable to slander.
- Accepting lesser professional success/lesser pay.
- Being a doormat, easily manipulated and deceived.
- Negative inner dialogue.
- Perfectionism and procrastination.
- Seeking power and control through violence.
- Failure and Loss of Goals.
- Attracting bullies.
- Lack of Fulfillment.
- Chronic Gossiping and Complaining.
- Aggression and Violence.
- Self-Judgment.
- Self-Betrayal.
- Self-Abandonment.
- Self-Loathing.
- Self-Denial and Deprivation.
- Self-Sacrifice.
- Attracting Abusers, Narcissists, Sociopaths and
  Psychopaths.
- Addiction and Self-medicating.

- Incarceration.
- Loss of Self/Identity Crisis.

There is a time in your life when you were able to suppress your shadow that you didn't even know it's there. As the years pass, the shadow begins to peek its head. It reveals itself gradually, but you don't think much of it. Others blame it on a phase in your life.

As it gains momentum, it gives birth to your inner demons. You were not prepared for this. You thought they will go away on their own, so you didn't arm yourself .

When faced with a choice, you either sit yourself down with your demons, or you become a ticking bomb. Without a truce, a nervous breakdown ensues. There is no more negotiating or bargaining. You cannot afford to ignore it any longer.

How dominant is your Shadow? Are you ready to cast your light onto the dark corners of your mind?

* * *

SHADOW ARCHETYPES

WE COULD each fit in more than one Shadow Archetype, with one being dominant. While they seem initially negative, they can be turned inside out into a valuable blueprint for self-knowledge that leads to integration and healing.

 "Know thyself and know thy measure." ~Socrates

THE FOLLOWING ARE Shadow Archetypes according to Dr. Carl Jung:

- The Sorcerer
- The Dictator
- The Victim
- The Shadow Witch
- The Addict
- The Idiot
- The Trickster
- The Destroyer
- The Slave
- The Shadow Mother
- The Hag
- The Hermit
- The Orphan

EXAMPLE: **THE ORPHAN**

The orphan archetype represents reckless givers, who deplete themselves to appease others. Unknowingly, the orphan's need to belong makes them mask the value they take from others under the guise of giving. Because they are reliable, they attract takers, who will take advantage of their loneliness and fear of abandonment. They try to join others in fear of being left out. Sometimes, they appear somber and awkward, and go into isolation when emotionally fatigued and disappointed. Once they hit rock bottom, they begin to change, take care of themselves, and attract better friends.

Goal: to belong

Fear: to be left out or to be the odd one out.

Weakness: can be a little too cynical

Talent: honest and open, pragmatic and realistic.

· · ·

THIS IS MY LIST OF SHADOW ARCHETYPES:

- The Scapegoat
- The Martyr
- The Narcissist
- The Pariah
- The Assassin (Abuser)
- The Paranoid Shadow
- The Judge
- The Green-eyed Monster
- The Devious Shadow
- The Traitor
- The Coward
- The Gossiping Shadow
- The Fanatic

Example in-depth analysis: THE SCAPEGOAT

This Archetype is the black sheep of the family; vulnerable to abuse and bullying. They, in turn, sacrifice themselves for others, to avoid abuse. Their deepest need is to be needed, because they think it will make them accepted and safe. The false belief that people don't destroy those they need subjects them to more abuse. People often destroy the ones they need to keep them small and useful, and to prevent them from seeing their worth. The Scapegoat gives without discrimination. They run on empty. They help others realize their dreams, while abandoning their own. When they recognize this dynamic, they learn that they are not genuine givers. They take value by sacrifice, and by attempting to buy people's love, which often leaves them depleted, disappointed, and resentful. Their resentment becomes the catalyst for developing clear boundaries. Slowly, they learn to set them, which causes them anxiety. Many try to guilt trip and manipulate them to continue using them. They hold the acceptance carrot just out of the scapegoat's reach. When the orphan holds his/her ground, they go through a period of stagnation, slowly turn their life around to face the right direction and fulfill their own dreams. They finally begin to invite healthier people into their lives, and feel repulsed by fake, opportunistic people. They no longer tolerate toxicity from themselves or from others.

Life Goal: To be needed, to be relevant, to be worthy, to avoid abuse and bullying.

Fear: Severe fear of abandonment, rejection, and ostracism.

Motivation: To receive kindness and love, to be protected, to be included, to receive empathy, to be saved.

Response to Problem: They sacrifice their wants and needs to fulfill those of others; they use fawning to avoid abuse; they lose their voice in fear of retaliation; they mentally escape to their safe space; they lose the sense of time and reality; they are unable to be fully present due to the preoccupation with fear of impending harm. They don't trust others and think the world is a dangerous place; they can become suicidal, or resort to self-harm.

Life Task: To parent oneself; to connect with inherent worth; to escape dangerous environments and avoid abusive people; to channel deep wounds into creative work; to be of service to other survivors; to extract value from within.

The Martyr

Life Goal: To avoid self-responsibility; to extract value from others by remaining stuck in helplessness and chaos.

Fear: Being inadequate and unloved.

Motivation: To receive attention and inspire pity.

Response to Problem: Blames external forces. Gets addicted to tuning in to dystopian news to justify own shortcomings and validate their helplessness.

Life Task: To take accountability for one's own life and to tap into their power.

Personal Gifts: Humanitarian; charity; advocation for positive change; promotes kindness. They learn to give to themselves so they give to others authentically.

* * *

THE NARCISSIST

Life Goal: To be acknowledged; validated; celebrated, and admired.

Fear: To be exposed; fear of abandonment; fear of judgment; fears accountability, blame and resents intimacy.

Motivation: To minimize self-loathing, insecurities.

Response to Problem: They split (black & white thinking/idealization and devaluation); manipulates and exploits others; projects own shortcomings on others; perfectionism.

Life Task: To channel talents into service; find careers that feed narcissism in a less damaging way, or even positively, such as the entertainment industry.

Personal Gifts: Charm through communication and creative expression; adaptability/chameleon like; charisma; presence; and spontaneity.

* * *

THE PARIAH

Life Goal: Liberation from social custom and tradition; living life on the edge; seeking adventure and adrenalin rushes, are often adrenalin junkies and/or criminals.

Fear: To be controlled, or incarcerated. They choose being outcasts before they are forced to be. They resent authority figures, and the timid alike.

Motivation: To be the dictator of rules; to remain free and unapproachable. To break boredom. To be significant.

Response to Problem: Trouble makers, extremists, risky behavior, poor impulse control; restlessness that can turn into violence. Rebellion is a sign of caring too much for others' approval, opinions, and attention. Negative attention is better than no attention at all. If they can't be famous, they become infamous.

Life Task: To turn risky behavior into healthy, fun adventure; to channel violent impulses into sports; to convert power struggles into finding own path. To stop caring what others think so it doesn't come out as defiance. **Personal Gifts:** Critical thinking; trend setters, adventurous; joie de vivre; creative minds. They can help liberate and empower others.

* * *

THE ASSASSIN

Life Goal: To control others; to extract power by victimizing others; to intimidate.

Fear: To be abandoned; to be disrespected.

Motivation: To be heard; to feel significant.

Response to Problem: Abusing others; use of violence to exert and keep power position; assassination of others' character. Cold-hearted and callous.

Life Task: To heal own shame; to extract power from within; to learn self-mastery, and presence of mind.

Personal Gifts: Leadership; charisma; passion.

THE PARANOID SHADOW

Life Goal: To be safe.

Fear: To lose sense of safety; to be betrayed; to be unable to meet basic needs for survival; to lose stability.

Motivation: To protect oneself and loved ones; to keep own life intact; to prevent disaster, to mask their fear.

Response to Problem: They become distrustful, and on guard; warn others of their severe punishment for betrayal; they go to any length to weaken or kill off a perceived enemy; they demonize others; they expect the worst; they initiate betrayal to avoid being betrayed. They often become tyrants.

Life Task: To refrain from assumptions; take well-thought out actions; minimize impulsivity; give others a chance to respond with their truth; to learn that intimidation reveals fear; to learn grounded communication, and exercise active listening.

Personal Gifts: Leadership skills; efficiency; can turn chaos into order; has strong values, and code of ethics when balanced.

* * *

THE JUDGE

Life Goal: To avoid exposing own shortcomings and silence own insecurities; to avoid feeling shame. Focus on others' flaws.

Fear: To be judged, and exposed.

Motivation: To be invulnerable to criticism. To belong and be accepted by the community.

Response to Problem: They gossip, slander, and point out the negative in everyone.

Life Task: To accept our flawed nature, and to forgive oneself for them.

Personal Gifts: Discernment, analytical, sharp.

* * *

THE VINDICTIVE SHADOW

Life Goal: To seek revenge on all perceived enemies.

Fear: To be attacked, disrespected, disobeyed, betrayed, and compromised.

Motivation: To gain power and control.

Response to Problem: Plotting against others, retaliation, and sabotage.

Life Task: To recognize the enemy within, and make amends. To replace false sense of power with authenticity. To learn that revenge poisons the avenger first and foremost.

Personal Gifts: Calculating master-mind when put to good use.

* * *

THE GREEN-EYED MONSTER

Life Goal: To remove other people's blessings. To have control over others. To lessen their own sense of worthlessness.

Fear: To live in scarcity. To never have or be enough.

Motivation: To take what isn't theirs; prevent others from having what they can't.

Response to Problem: They envy others; wishing away someone's blessings. Jealousy that leads to possessiveness of a person or a thing. Resentment towards others for having what they lack.

Life Task: To learn gratitude, and to recognize own blessings. To stop focusing on scarcity. Learn to appreciate without willing destruction on others; allow oneself to be inspired. To nurture own garden.

Personal Gifts: Passion and focus. Energetic powers. They can channel their powerful energy into healing others.

* * *

THE MAGICIAN

Life Goal: To manipulate and deceive others. To evade accountability.

Fear: They fear confrontation due to cowardice. They think they have to manipulate others to get what they want.

Motivation: To avoid accountability, and to receive what they want without directly asking for it.

Response to Problem: They deceive; use passive-aggressive methods. They resent those, who ask them for favors.

Life Task: To learn how to ask for help, and not judge themselves for it. To know life is give and take.

Personal Gifts: They are charming, and creative thinkers. Once they stop manipulating others, they can channel their chameleon-like qualities into creative work.

* * *

THE TRAITOR

Life Goal: Disguising themselves as friends, to gain trust then to betray others for personal gain.

Fear: They fear confrontation, loss and rejection.

Motivation: To be a few steps ahead of others. They fear competition. They use others as stepping stones with no regard or reciprocity.

Response to Problem: They make themselves seem available and supportive. They overshare to speed up intimacy. They take up all of their target's time and energy, to have exclusive access to resources. They give as a way to control and create debt.

Life Task: To become one's friend. Betrayal of others is a telling sign of self-betrayal. To learn that true friendship gets you much farther than any betrayal ever will.

Personal Gifts: Adaptable and witty.

* * *

THE COWARD

Life Goal: To avoid accountability, confrontation and blame; to get attention by disappearing; to avoid being exposed by demonizing others; to slander those, who see through the behavior. They make others reach a boiling point so they can assert their victim position.

Fear: To be reprimanded, or asked for help.

Motivation: Evade responsibility and admission of guilt.

Response to Problem: They hide real emotions and intentions; are hypocritical, evasive, resentful, and deceptive. They underhandedly sabotage others and paint themselves as heroes or martyrs. They cheat, lie and steal with no regard for others.

Life Task: To learn passive-aggression is most damaging, and acquire communication skills; to learn saying a simple no, instead of causing damage to others and the relationship; to be comfortable in uncomfortable conversations to avoid explosive retaliation from others.

Personal Gifts: Fun loving, and engaging, if behaviour is genuinely healed.

THE GOSSIPING SHADOW

Life Goal: To debase others to raise oneself. To dig up dirt and to advertise it. To receive pleasure from others' pain.

Fear: To be exposed; to be disgraced; to face own inferiority.

Motivation: To silence own insecurities; to avert negative attention.

Response to Problem: Engages in slander, bullying, inspires hatred, creates drama, betrays trust, manipulates others, obsesses over other people's perceived strength.

Life Task: To nurture own strengths and talents; to learn self-love and self-respect; to heal own pain and address own insecurities; to value oneself and one's time and energy.

Personal Gifts: Fun loving, and engaging, if behaviour is genuinely healed. Are potential humanitarians, if empathy is acquired. They can raise awareness on important causes, or help generate positive publicity.

The Fanatic

Life Goal: To belong; to have an identity; identity tied with beliefs; to control by force

Fear: Loss of identity; to be an outcast, loss of power

Motivation: To change others; to enforce own identity on others; to shame others; extracting validation and confirmation by converting others into carbon copies of their fragmented self.

Response to Problem: Terrorism; crimes under the guise of ideologies and religion; inspiring hatred and wars.

Life Task: To untangle self-value, and self-worth from beliefs. Find security in solitude; extracting validation from within.

Personal Gifts: Passion; heroism channeled positively; loyalty; faithfulness.

Which one/s do you identify with? Are you willing to turn your shadow's control into authentic power?

* * *

CHAPTER 5
COMPLEX TRAUMA

The moment you were awakened to what you are,
all of the traumas became distant stories.
Everything you have been told, and all you
have seen are now nothing but a prehensile
dream.

Types of Trauma

These are the two types of traumas I will be covering in this chapter, with a focus on the complex kind due to its emotional roots and prolonged nature. It is not necessarily the trauma itself that causes long-term problems, but the impact of how others re-traumatize a person that keeps them stuck. We can move on from an event.

When society keeps you entrapped in its memory, your struggle is that much tougher.

1. Post-traumatic stress disorder
2. Complex post-traumatic stress disorder

* * *

PTSD vs. C-PTSD

PTSD is a manifestation of one traumatic event, as is the case for war veterans, one time rape victims, loss of a loved one, being diagnosed with a serious illness, witnessing or being involved in an accident. C-PTSD is a result of ongoing, compounded trauma, mostly rooted in emotional abuse caused by "trusted" caretakers and loved ones.

When anxiety is a constant state, our bodies slowly give out. Code red is an expected norm. This is why when we rage, we refer to it as seeing red. C-PTSD brings everything dangerous from the past right into the present moment. We create mental scenarios of impending doom, so we can be on high alert, should we need to protect ourselves and act fast enough.

The absence of immediate danger only intensifies the anticipation. It is equivalent to the anxiety you feel between the time someone points a gun at you, and pulling the trigger. Sufferers of C-PTSD are in a constant state of survival mode. Their trauma is timeless, and their mind can't organize their memories in a chronological order. Everything is happening inside at the same time.

Being in the now is the ultimate state that spiritual guides talk about, but what if the moment is unpleasant? This is when mentally escaping the moment comes to save us, and we replace it with another. This is when people either meditate or dissociate. Trauma weakens the mind, and meditation fortifies it. Mind over matter is not always a capacity that the sufferer has. Instead, they dissociate, because it does not require effort. It is not intentional. There is a fine line between the height of pain and a complete liberation from it.

Adrenalin kicks in, prompting us into fight, flight, freeze or fawn mode. Being high on adrenalin consistently is physically exhausting to say the least. Since our emotional memory gets stored in our bodies, we become heavy. The reason we tend to suppress our traumatic memories is to avoid being driven into a nervous breakdown, or sometimes, suicide. I do believe; however, in taking small steps to release little by little, with a hiatus in between for processing. Every person is different, so you will have to decide on the best course of action for you with the help of a trusted professional. If you choose to keep your emotions bottled up, sooner or later they will express themselves through unexpected ways, at unexpected times, without your consent. It can often awaken fatal diseases, just to get your attention.

SYMPTOMS OF C-PTSD

- Derealization
- Dissociation
- Blocked memory
- Non-linear recalling of events
- Forgetting a familiar face
- Seeing others' face change into someone else
- Failure to feel moments, even while engaged in them
- Feeling unsettled when someone is behind you
- Need to protect your back, yet needing to look away from others at times
- Sleeping in clothes you can run out in at any moment
- Slow response time due to dissociation
- May take a couple of weeks to realize someone insulted you and you didn't react at the time
- You may see and hear things that aren't quite there.
- Inability to defend yourself due to memory blockages.
- Loud noises, hard lights, and crowds hurt your senses and give you anxiety.
- Vertigo is common. Sometimes you cannot see anything but bright white light. You are briefly blind.

- There is a deep distrust in people and fear of loss.
- Paranoia

 "Dude, I've been seeing things that aren't there. The last thing I need is paranoia."Hurley
"I just shot a man, who's been sitting outside your window for the past week. I'm finding paranoia keeps me alive." Sayid Jarrah ~LOST/J.J. Abrams

* * *

Causes of C-PTSD

Causes of C-PTSD: (Complex Post Traumatic Stress Disorder), often misdiagnosed as Borderline Personality Disorder, and therefore, causes more harm to the patients when prescribed with the wrong medications. Left untreated, patients become more prone to triggers.

Below is a list of possible causes of Complex Trauma:

- Childhood emotional abuse.
- Inconsistent upbringing.
- Neglect.
- Loss of a parent, or both.
- Loss of a child.
- Physical Abuse.
- Unsafe and/or Unsupportive upbringing.
- Childhood sexual abuse especially if done by a family member.
- Victims of kidnapping, rape, human trafficking, stalking, and false imprisonment.
- Social ostracism
- Victim shaming.
- Character assassination and public humiliation.
- Domestic Violence.

- Childhood abandonment.
- Abusive relationships and friendships.
- Gaslighting (crazy-making behavior by invalidating your reality)
- Cheating and betrayal by a romantic partner/spouse.
- Repeated heartbreak and victims of love fraud.

C-PTSD sufferers are 80% more prone to further abuse by more abusers, if left untreated. Due to the little understanding of the condition, they are often abandoned by their support network and mental health professionals. Therapists who force the sufferer to speak may mirror their traumatic experience, if it was related to oppression of any kind. Often, they appear balanced, healthy and high functioning. Victim shaming greatly intensifies the trauma; its traces make them easy prey for predators. We can heal much faster, if further abuse by judgment is not present. Empathy is critical to healing.

Note: Abandonment isn't always physical. Some parents are around their children, yet can't manage to be present with them. It can be through denying them attention, invalidating their emotions, neglecting the child's needs, and dismissal of the child's thoughts.

TRAUMA BONDING

Trauma bonding is the deepest form of bonding, which develops between the predator and the prey; the abuser and the abused. As the abuse escalates, victims are firmly locked in psychologically, and the tie to their abuser is solidified. It is often used interchangeably with Stockholm Syndrome; however, I believe a slight discernment would be in order. A trauma bond implies one created by prolonged abuse by a kidnapper, a romantic partner, or a family member with whom the victim lives, or is in a long term relationship with.

STOCKHOLM SYNDROME IS term that was coined due to an incident of a bank robbery in Stockholm, when those held hostage empathized with the robber, because he demonstrated acts of kindness. It can occur in a one-off incident. In the next chapter, there is more on Stockholm Syndrome specifically. Whether it is trauma bonding or Stockholm Syndrome, random or calculated acts of kindness are the catalyst for both conditions. Abusers use intermittent reinforcement, because it rapidly creates a solid bond that is tough to break. Victims are not necessarily physically held hostage. Sometimes, they are psychologically and spiritually captured to such a degree that they are free to move, yet remain compliant to the abuser. It is as though they have an invisible, tight leash that forces them to return. This is one of the main reasons it is not easy to just leave. I am using a female example for the victim, and a male for the abuser, but please note the genders can be reversed.

VICTIM'S PROFILE:

- Spiritual and empathetic
- Kindness, and forgiveness are main features.
- Gullible.
- Prone to feel guilt.
- Often intelligent, successful, joyful, and strong.
- Hopeless romantic, sees the best in others, while ignoring red flags.
- Enjoys being led by her partner.
- Doesn't have a solid support system.
- Emotionally broken or lonely.

HERE ARE SOME WAYS TO BREAK THE TRAUMA BOND:

- *See the abuser for who he is, rather than the aggrandized image he projects.*
- *Sometimes, overindulging in an addiction makes us develop and aversion to it. You can invest fully into the abuser until you reach this state, which gives you strength to leave.*
- *Reconnect with yourself.*
- *Treat it as a drug you need to quit.*
- *Do not project your good qualities onto an abuser. Sporadic kindness should not exonerate someone of their abusive and violent behaviour.*

MODUS OPERANDI OF TRAPPING VICTIMS

- Initial charm and whirlwind romance.
- A sob story used as a ruse to make her think he's vulnerable, open and trustworthy.
- She feels special that he can confide in her, not realizing he will later triangulate her with the same people he once trashed.
- He compliments her, and offers her advice to test her boundaries, and see how he can influence her.
- The control increases; he takes up her time, attention, and consumes her energy to deplete and isolate her.
- Isolation can be physical, mental or emotional. He damages her most important relationships. This can be done covertly or overtly.
- If sulking works, he uses it frequently to modify her behavior.
- He attacks her confidence and self-worth under the guise of care and advice, which escalates to firm orders.
- They instill paranoia and doubt to make her believe

that others don't like her/talk negatively about her
behind her back.

- He uses intermittent reinforcement to confuse her,
  and keep her hopeful. He will get hot and cold; his
  anger will be followed by love bombing. He knows
  this creates addiction.
- He systematically kills her spirit, confidence,
  radiance, hopes and dreams.

When the unhealed parts of ourselves are driving us into
dangerous situations, it is due to our perceived inability to
escape or defend ourselves. If, in our childhood, we were abused
in any way, the behavior is normalized in our subconscious,
even if we can intellectualize the wrongness of the situation.

Anyone can be subjected to abuse; however, those carrying
old wounds are more prone to attracting it, which makes it
more complicated to break free. Once we heal from within,
getting rid of abusers and toxic people in general becomes
simpler.

Repetition Compulsion

> If only we can get that impossible person to love
> us, we can have hope our parents will love us
> too. But we cannot retrieve a past love by
> proxy.

When we can't get love and attention from our caregivers,
we look for others that will mirror their dynamic, and hope we
can fix it this time around. History does not have to repeat
itself. When we create an inexplicably deep bond with someone,
who abuses us, we may be recreating an old narrative we were
subjected to in childhood. We feel comfortable in the old

dynamic because it is what we have grown to know. Our tolerance for toxic patterns creates a blindspot to abuse.

We do not recognize it as such. We confuse violence for love, and associate pain with pleasure. Everyone has patterns, which keep repeating, unless there is a conscious decision to discontinue manufacturing it. The comfort zone tends to be the most damaging. We get addicted to our old stories, and to familiarity. No matter how bad it is, we perceive it as better than the unknown. Who are you without your story?

 "Just give me a pain that I'm used to."~Depeche Mode

LEARNED HELPLESSNESS

Early trauma is the perfume we wear that attracts
    more predators.

When we are children, exposed to any form of abuse, with no one to protect us, we become conditioned to be helpless. We may not be able to respond to abuse, because our mind still believes we are unable to defend ourselves as grown ups. Some abuse is hidden like childhood sexual abuse. Overt abuse is often the type caregivers shrug off, such as sibling on sibling violence. Learned helplessness is behind a deer-in-headlights response.

CHILDHOOD SEXUAL ABUSE

To everyone else, summer meant holiday, but to
    her, it was rape season.

A rapist feels unworthy of getting positive attention, so they have to get it by stealing it. Intercourse is a powerful gateway into one's core energy, and soul. It violates the body, and one's energetic being. Psychic attacks are a real thing, and the most powerful and fastest way to infiltrate another person is through their sacral chakra. The sacral chakra is the gateway to our emotional body; it is home for creativity and sensuality. Its element is water. Being violated in this manner cuts through the doors that protect your soul. The child, who is being violated will not have the language or the awareness to know what is happening to them. They instinctively know something wrong is happening, yet their body is responding with inexplicable pleasure. This, alone, creates deep shame, and cognitive dissonance, which push them into silence.

When, on rare occasions, children report to their parent of what happened, they are often shamed, yelled at, and accused of lying. Due to the absence of protection, the child quickly learns that being helpless should be expected. They carry shame throughout their life, unless they deal with the initial trauma.

Predators leave prints on their victims that other predators can detect from a distance. Victims grow to believe they must deserve it, and fear telling anyone in fear of dismissal and judgment. In some countries, law enforcement would look down on the victim, and prevent them from bringing the rapist to justice.

Society prosecutes females for what males are praised for. The shame women carry for their bodies make them vulnerable to sexual predators, and then being shunned for it. The fact that most people doing the shaming are also women is what makes such a trauma even more tragic. The callousness of some people is beyond comprehension. Male victims experience deep shame, because they rarely discuss their history of sexual abuse. When a boy is violated, he will be shamed for it and accused of being a homosexual. If their attacker was an older female, their feelings of being violated is dismissed. Instead, others may think it's something to be proud of. In any event, it is the social reaction to abuse that prolongs its impact.

Impact of Trauma

> Many of us are emotional third-degree burn
> victims. Breathe gently in the opposite
> direction.

The impact of trauma can take a life of its own. We are fortunate to have many incredible tools for healing. Being mindful of who we surround ourselves with during our recovery makes a world of difference. We are all traumatized in one way or another, which should be reason enough to make us understand and empathize with each other. Understanding is not even a pre-requisite to kindness. We don't have to wait for someone to die to love them properly. Everything becomes clear in hindsight. Anyone can tell you what you should have done instead. Therefore, 20/20 advice is not of much use.

 "We are here to help each other remember, and then let go."~Inspired by LOST

1. Dissociation

When you are in the middle of a traumatic event with no help in sight, you dissociate. Your mind will leave to a safer space. You split. It is the only option to survive. Dissociation can be temporary during a traumatic event, or becomes an involuntary habit. It gets easily triggered. When there is any resemblance, no matter how faint, to a past trauma, dissociation goes into effect. Some people may take a couple of weeks before they realize they've been insulted, and decide to react long after the incident. Sometimes, it gets triggered by a pleasant situation in the presence of an abuser. If the abuser is in a good mood, they can still trigger anxiety in the victim, as they never know what the next moment can bring. So, they may miss out on moments. Moreover, preoccupation with trauma can lead to dissociation in casual situations. The normalcy of the people around may act as a reminder of how flawed the person is, and how they are unable to feel any real sense of belonging. Kindness in others may be a trigger as victims of abuse are conditioned that pleasantness and niceness are usually followed by harm. The show of kindness in others acts as a red flag to those, who were subjected by intermittent reinforcement.

2. DEREALIZATION

I wish I could realize I am here, but I'm not sure
I am.

It's a kind of a funny feeling to be in a moment without being in it. People appear like cartoon characters. Nothing seems to be real. I suppose it's a state that many have to smoke something to understand it. Trauma creates all kinds of mental highs and low, and this one can be, both, fun and painful. Anticipating a desired moment, only to miss out on it when it arrives can be heartbreaking when it's gone. You realize later that you didn't get to enjoy it, because your mind was anxious and preoccupied with the inevitable pain that will come when it is over. You get consumed by your fears, and life flows in and out with you unaware. There is an invisible bubble around you and everyone else seems just out of your reach. Knowing that everything comes to an end, you subconsciously refrain from fully investing in a moment of joy, thinking it may lessen the pain that comes up at the moment of departure. But when that moment comes, you regret missing out on it, while it was there now that it's gone. Lean into it, because the pain of loss is more bearable when it is not combined with the pain of regret.

3. Quasi Accidents

Being an accident prone is a way of self-harm
without being held accountable for anything
except clumsiness.

Traumas caused by prolonged or ongoing emotional abuse gets us out of alignment, and not much care is given to our safety. When we feel perpetually unsafe, our minds become unfocused, disorganized and fragmented. We become prone to accidents. It can be a moment of dissociation, derealisation, or a subconscious need to make ourselves escape a painful reality. Due to the intense preoccupation with the trauma, we may not see cars coming, or a ditch in the road. Maybe, on a subconscious level, we want to make ourselves less appealing to predators, and hope one of those accidents would prove fatal, as it is often perceived to be the only refuge from a life of constant terror.

4. Vertigo

Listen to your body when it objects.

Our bodies know what's dangerous before our minds begin to fathom it. Vertigo can be caused by an imbalance of the inner ear, a heart or brain issue. But there is also stress related vertigo. Trauma certainly can bring on episodes of vertigo when we are overwhelmed or in the presence of someone with an intensely dark energy. It is an overload for a traumatized mind to be hypnotized by someone's charisma, yet their body senses danger. We get dizzy, and sick due to the cognitive dissonance. It is disorienting. Vertigo is a great indicator to dangerous people long before they plan to reveal themselves to you.

Our bodies have intuitive intelligence that, if we only listen to it, we will come to find that we had access to all the information we ever needed all along. I found truth within my vertigo. People can be charming and funny, both of which are powerful characteristics to cover up malicious intentions. We can experience vertigo to be warned of an energetic vampire before us; take it as a signal to remove yourself from their presence.

* * *

MENTAL DIS-EASE

    "*It is no measure of health to be well adjusted to a profoundly sick society.*"~*Jiddu Krishnamurti*

WHAT IS MENTAL ILLNESS, and who decides what's Insane?
Categorizing people by the level of their sanity is something I'm unable to come to terms with. It has been evident that we are not primarily rational beings. Logic, outside of certain sciences, is subjective. The mind is designed to fill in the blanks. When we hear stories, we add our interpretations and rationalizations to them. We embellish and diminish, which makes objectivity tough to achieve. According to Buddhism, being out of our mind is a good thing. It allows us to connect with our soul rather than our ego that promotes self-consciousness and self-obsession.

Common sense refers to the integration of our senses and alignment to reach common ground within ourselves, and not about a common collective sense. It is not possible given we are subjectively unique. Some may strive to share common senses and logic by complying to social custom and by abandoning their individuality in the name of fitting in. If we attach the meaning of common sense to the collective, we continue to break our minds trying to wonder where it has gone. Find common ground within you rather than losing your balance into the inevitable earthquake of a shared psychosis.

> We are all masters of rationalizing our behaviors
> and will find justifications, if we can't.

What is logical to you may not be logical to another. Since logic is evidence based, many people can't see logic in what they have not experienced first hand. When entire civilizations normalize wars, fast food, monetizing the planet, creating borders between countries and all kinds of lovely things, wouldn't that make us engage in a shared psychosis? If those perceived as healthy have an incredible level of self-deception, project on each other unaware, and have a hard time breaking old patterns, how do we expect rationality, let alone sanity?

The human mind is complicated and highly prone to subjectivity. Sometimes I refer to life as a long psychedelic experience. Some readers will affirm my view, while others will call me utterly insane.

Jim Carey has divided opinions between having lost his mind and having been awakened. To me, he did indeed awaken to what was previously dormant within him, but the fact that he is eager to share it with the world may be telling of the excitement of new awareness. Once he settles into it, he will rise to the next level of inspiring others without imposition, and without the complete denial of the current reality. Sure, this reality is ultimately a projection and it is as real as we make it, but it does not make it any less worthy of acknowledgement while we are in it. Once we box people and things into a label we become blind to all other aspects of them.

Today, we celebrate people, who were sent into exile and pronounced insane in their time. Sanity to one can be insane to another. One man's insanity is another man's genius.

We are insane until proven genius.

This is not to discount the field of psychoanalysis; in fact, I am a firm believer in psychology's important role in our lives. I am using the medical labels/diagnosis for the sake of clarity, but I do so begrudgingly. It helps to understand personality types, to know how to deal with them, rather than judging them. Many people today call everyone around them a narcissist as though it were an insult. It is an understandable phenomenon; I am guilty of it myself. I only hope we take better care that we refrain from imprisoning others within a diagnosis or an opinion so we can see them fully rather than through the murky lens of limitations.

Cluster B personalities behave in appalling ways. Having a diagnosis of a disorder does not justify malice and utter disregard for others' well-being. Psychopaths are born this way, and so, their mental illness makes it more tricky to hold them accountable. It is still our collective responsibility to admit that the world is often mimicking psychopathic behavior. It used to be the other way around. Some are not born a psychopath, yet behave with the same level of malice. Glorifying psychopathic behavior is a bigger threat to humanity than the threat imposed by your average career criminal. Psychopathic predators, and their groupies, mostly, appear friendly, charming, attractive and well-educated. Their weapon is in their perfect mask. They are mistaken for good friends, and even loyal family members. No wonder, we are all becoming distrustful. When we become collectively paranoid, we create a whole new set of challenges. We now need to avoid the wrath and false accusations of the paranoid man, who rages just to silence his excessive fears.

Cognitive Dissonance

The disease of our time is cognitive dissonance.

Cognitive Dissonance is holding two opposing beliefs simultaneously. It is when what we want is in sharp contrast to what we believe. It creates great discomfort in the mind, which is why people eventually drop a behavior that conflicts with their beliefs, or drop the belief to further indulge in the behavior without guilt.

THE TIME it takes to drop one or the other can be stretched. They sway between the pursuit of pleasure, and the guilt that follows the next moment. People, who are broken-minded will often blame the object of their desire, rather than condemning themselves for desiring it. Blame shifting and projection softens the intensity of their mental anguish.

In religious communities, whose teachings are heavily built on shame and fear, people are divided between their desires and their beliefs. In permissive communities, they tend to naturally refrain from extremist behaviors.

DEPRIVATION INTENSIFIES THE DESIRE. Cognitive dissonance is tough to reconcile, because most people aren't aware of their mental divide. They deny, project, rationalize and justify. Once we become aware of the areas that makes us divided, we can make a conscious choice to drop a behaviour or a belief.

Dropping damaging beliefs prompts us to naturally drop our extreme ways.

* * *

The Psychology of Desire

> We have the freedom to pursue whatever we
> desire, but we don't have the freedom to choose
> that which we desire.

The shadow makes us blind to our true heart's desires. When desires are inspired within us, they happen naturally. We don't decide to desire something or someone. We don't understand the process. However, I do believe we can master our desires, by understanding our true motivations. Since we are mainly either motivated by what we fear or by what we love, we must lift the darkness one layer at a time. We can then eliminate the desires that were motivated by fear through dealing with our demons. What we will be left with are the higher desires that help us fulfill our divine calling.

The following often inspire our desire:

1. Our innate preferences. We desire aloneness, because we fear socialization, or desire social activity, because we fear being alone.

2. Fear can steer us into opposition, by desiring something in fear of its opposite. We may desire wealth, because we fear being powerless, and desire failure, because we fear criticism. This can be equally evident during elections, when people vote for someone, because they fear or dislike the other candidate a bit more.

3. We can feel a pull toward a person, who resembles our

early family dynamics. Maybe this person resembles a parent we have unfinished business with, and mimics their attachment style. We may not know why we desire this person, until they expose our core wounds.

WHAT IF WE are no longer driven by our fears, would we have the same desires? If we do, what would they feel like coming from a higher motivation of the heart? What new desires will be revealed, and which will die along with the demon that hosted it? Who are you without your fear? What would you allow yourself to desire?

CONFIRMATION BIAS

Confirm what I want to acknowledge, and
confirm the falsehood of what I want to deny.

Confirmation Bias is when someone refuses and denies any evidence that does not support their beliefs, no matter how strong the evidence is. There is a fear behind every stubborn stance. When we identify ourselves with our ideologies, we fear being exposed to perspectives that may threaten our reality. Fear of loss is a major player in confirmation bias. If you allow others to present new evidence that goes against your belief about it, or your comfort zone, you fear losing your right to keep doing whatever you were doing. Haters engage in narrow-mindedness whenever someone shows evidence of positive qualities in the same person they are hating on. They simply refuse to accept it. They continue to find fault. We can all recall an instance when we had to go to great lengths to prove our innocence to someone, who refused to budge from what they believed about us. What they gain out of it may be too good to give up, and the loss is too great, should they change their mind. For example, if someone's best interest is to demonize you, they will be relentless in rejecting any positive trait about you. People are often self-serving, and are skilled at justifying a behavior for personal gain. It is ignorance of convenience.

Jury Members

> Either we are all guilty or we are all innocent. To indict the one calls for the indictment of all. To exonerate one is to exonerate the rest.

The jury system always fascinated me, and I used to wish we had court procedures that are as fun and interesting as they do in the US. The movies certainly make it exciting, and America is great at making some cases sensational, as it was with Ted Bundy, "The Green River Killer", O.J.Simpson, "The Menendez Brothers" and now, everyone is awaiting R. Kelly's fate, whose character has been, indeed, assassinated before he could face a jury.

The dangers of publicity is how quick the general public is to indict or exonerate with little knowledge of human psychology in general, and criminal psychology in particular. The judge is the ultimate decision-maker in the sentencing, but guilt and innocence are often placed in untrained hands. Lawyers and prosecutors are often fixated on a story-telling match rather than what is fair. The innocent verdict for O.J.Simpson jolted millions of people into shock, including, his late attorney and long time friend, Robert Kardashian. The blood evidence was trumped by unfitting, crime scene gloves, which Mr. Simpson was trying on over latex gloves as opposed to the regular way of trying them on... without latex gloves. *"If it didn't fit, you must acquit."* Johnnie Cochran powerfully said this, just before earning his client an innocent verdict.

Following this case, came the murder of Kitty and her husband, José Menendez, a former tycoon in the music and film industries in Hollywood. The ones who pulled the triggers are their two sons, Lyle, 21 at the time, and Eric, 19. However, the ones, who pulled the symbolic trigger were the parents by their years of abuse and neglect.

SENSATIONAL CASES, used and abused by the media, turn the general public into judges and jurors. If in the U.S.A everyone has a constitutional right to a fair trial, then there has to be a law that protects privacy until the verdict is decided through the legal system, rather than a public one. Jurors are chosen from the general public. While I'm sure it has its advantages, its disadvantages can have grave consequences on the defendants. In murder cases, pre-meditation is a main point of concern that will determine the degree of the crime, and the outcome. There is always the question of justification, as to know whether the killer was acting in self-defense or not. If jury members are not well-versed in human psychology, their verdict loses credibility. Complex trauma played a huge role in the Menendez trial, yet the jury decided their fate to spend their life behind bars.

* * *

THE MENENDEZ BROTHERS

The brothers were sexually, mentally, financially, and physically abused by their father José, while their mother, Kitty, was not doing anything about it, which is abuse by neglect and enabling behaviour. Instead, she numbed with alcohol and prescription drugs, while warning the boys against speaking up about secrets that would fragment and destroy the family. There was a perfect image to uphold, no matter the cost.

Much of the guilty verdict was due to lack of evidence to being in direct danger at the time of the crime, and the outrage that resulted from killing the mother. My issue with this is when children are subjected to prolonged abuse, they develop complex trauma. Sufferers of Complex Trauma live in a perpetual state of danger, which, in their mind, is always in the present. The abuser, José, followed through with his threats more often than not. It was enough to take any hint of threat seriously, and that day, José threatened Eric harm, should he tell anyone about the rape.

PEOPLE, who do not suffer prolonged abuse, lose their temper and presence of mind when cornered. Those with complex PTSD experience the same a million times over. José didn't even have to pose any threat on the day of the murders for the boys to feel unsafe. As for the murder of their mother, most people couldn't find any justification for her murder, which was the most inflammatory in everyone's eyes. Allowing abuse is still abuse. Those, who understood that, were heartbroken by the verdict and the subsequent separation of the young brothers. The thing about Kitty is that she perfectly fit the profile of a codependent, suffering abused wife syndrome. She was José's victim just as much; however, the boys shouldn't be expected to understand her complicity and failure to protect or support them. It may have been a bit of a gray area had José been only mentally or emotionally abusive, but to turn a blind eye to a husband, who is raping both his sons is what I found infuriating. Certainly, murder is never something to condone, yet since this is the fact, I believe it was the parents, who pulled the symbolic trigger first on these boys.

. . .

AFTER THE MURDERS/BEFORE ARREST

The following six months brought negative attention to the boys, who were previously not considered suspects. When they went on a lavish shopping spree, people, including the authorities, began to wonder if they had committed the crime. After their arrest, that shopping spree would prove detrimental. It painted them as callous and greedy. Once the motivation seems to be money, all abuse was thrown out the window. Shopping is a form of purging pain. Ask any shopaholic, and ask most women, who run to the mall whenever they feel heartbreak or anxiety.

In my heart, I do not believe the greed theory, nor can I blame them for what had transpired. Those boys do not belong in jail. I call them boys, because it bothered the prosecutor, who, creepily held on to Kitty's murder photo some 20 years later.

The term, "The abuse excuse" can easily trigger anger in those, who are indeed victims of abuse, which she often used. I call them boys, because their father trapped them in a painful boyhood, and I am glad to know they are, at least, reunited in the same prison last year. They are now grown men, happily married, and hopefully would be released, one day.

Some speculated that the Prosecutors' office needed to win a guilty verdict to make up for the embarrassing loss of the O.J. Simpson trial. Prosecutors were accused of being lenient on the rich and famous, and they had to prove everyone wrong.

* * *

SURVIVING/SCAPEGOATING R. KELLY

After watching "Surviving R. Kelly" one evening, it was deeply triggering. I cried, with the alleged victims...at first. But then another emotion came up, and that was confusion. Something wasn't right. So I dug deeper, within me, and the validity of the accusations. His character was feasted on, and to publicly assassinate him in this manner could compromise justice, wherever it lands.

I hope every victim turns into a survivor, and for every survivor to get justice. For justice to take place, we must weed out anyone, who makes false accusations. Sadly, a false victim causes great setbacks in this important cause. True victims, who are engaging in dodgy behavior, may obstruct justice for themselves and other survivors.

Gayle King's interview with R. Kelly took place after the documentary was released. Ms. King is always graceful and efficient. Her eyes are kind, even when she doubts someone's innocence. Since the interview, the whole world offered an opinion, a body language analysis, and even, a verdict. Anyone, who dabbles in psychology can understand that a nod means yes, and a head shake means no.

When Ms. King asked Mr. Kelly if he engaged in sexual activity with underage girls, he said no, while nodding. People rushed to take that as an inadvertent admission of guilt. However, when you are under massive attack, your character assassinated by many previously trusted people, and publicly at that, you can nod your head yes as a confirmation to your negation of guilt. Has anyone ever asked you a simple question, to which you responded no, and they kept asking if you are sure? At some point, you will get frustrated, say a resounding "NO" as you nod your head to make them believe you.

As for the head shake, when Ms. King asked him, "So, everyone is lying on you, everyone?" Mr. Kelly shook his head as he replied, "Absolutely". This can be a signal of his disbelief to the amount of people he was betrayed by. When he cried, they accused him of playing the victim and shedding crocodile tears. The fact that he has knowingly married a 15 year-old singer, is questionable. His severe dyslexia can make him easily deceived. Certainly, I am not defending him, but I am defending his right to tell his story, and his right to a fair trial.

Whether he is guilty or not, this will be for the courts and karma to decide; however, false victims severely hurt the ones, who truly suffer. Could this be a roundabout way to bring down the rapidly blooming MeToo movement that destroyed Weinstein? We shall see.

> Confirmation bias leads to great injustice, but everyone will get theirs in time. The Universe will always restore balance. But what if life is nothing but a trip, and we create conflict when someone is on a different substance than ours?

DRUGS ARCHETYPES

> In the freedom from one thing, one becomes enslaved by another.

Some drugs can create self-inflicted complex trauma when used excessively over a prolonged period of time. They change the brain pathways, and; therefore, can alter the personality. It is worth noting, that while substances can impact the wiring of the brain, and compromise our emotional responses, they cannot be blamed for someone's chosen methods of negative behavior. Substances bring out what's inside. Not everyone, who drinks, gets violent and not every coke-head is an ego-maniac. External chemicals interact with our own brain chemicals, and so results cannot be identical. What keeps you up could knock me down.

There may not be a specific, official, scientific link between a personality type and the drug of choice, but we often share observations of the most highlighted traits within each that we can use for character profiling. There are exceptions to every rule, so we will take a general look at the commonalities.

We are all addicted to one thing or another, and can relate to a wide array of emotional/mental states. Still, developing a character without any knowledge of the substance will make it overly dramatic, and shallow at best. You can be coached to inspire some effects via a natural high/low.

SIDE NOTE: Writers/Actors do not have to consume a drug to develop a character. The alternative, is to connect with the emotional motivations and mental states within yourself that are equivalent to what the drug user experiences.

HERE ARE SOME EXAMPLES:

COCAINE ARCHETYPES

Characteristics: Sociopathic and Narcissistic Traits. Tyranny, self-obsession, inflated sense of self, violence, overestimation of one's abilities, and underestimation of others.

Emotional Root Cause: They are ridden with suppressed insecurities, social anxiety, paranoia, self-loathing, fear of inadequacy and weakness.

Emotional goals: Confidence, emotional fortitude.

Positive traits: Sociability, and self-assuredness.

Negative traits: Leads to lack of empathy, isolation by psychosis or other forms of mental illness.

HEROIN ARCHETYPE

Characteristics: Borderline Personality traits, covert narcissism, histrionic personalities, introverted, yet could be exhibitionistic, hyper-sensitivity to emotional pain, high tolerance to physical pain. They are highly prone to hysteria, have lower inhibitions, and high risk taking behaviors.

Emotional Root Cause: Insecurity, fear of emotional pain, lack of self-worth, shame.

Emotional goals: Emotional numbness.

Positive traits: Empathy, kindness.

Negative traits: Selfishness, uselessness, pathological lying.

KETAMINE

Characteristics: Meditative, serene, and gentle.

Emotional Root Cause: Depression.

Emotional goals: Grounded, creative, and joyful.

Positive traits: Creativity and spiritual solutions.

Negative traits: Laziness, addictive behaviors, and codependency.

ECSTASY/MDMA

Characteristics: Borderline Personality traits, histrionic personalities, Bipolar traits.

Emotional Root Cause: Emotional pain, in need of love and affection.

Emotional goals: Synthetic love and happiness.

Positive traits: Love, joy, and connection with others.
Negative traits: Inconsistency and inauthenticity. Depression. Emotional roller-coaster.

ALCOHOL

Characteristics: Cluster B personality Disorders, Psychopathy, and Bipolar Disorder; naturally introverted or private, insecure, masking emotional pain, yet could be exhibitionistic, hyper-sensitive, has low tolerance to mental pain. They are highly prone to hysteria, have lower inhibitions, and high risk taking behaviors. Magnification of inner emotions.

Emotional Root Cause: Insecurity, anger, fear.

Emotional goals: Uninhibited and audacious.

Positive traits: Fun loving and good sense of humor.

Negative traits: Negligence, lack of accountability, violence, and refusal to admit guilt or face the music.

ADDICTION IS CAUSED by a loss of connection. All addictions are initially mental and emotional, before they become physical. We eat, buy, and drink the emotion we are lacking.

> *Show me your drug of choice, I'll show you what you*
> *fear and what you seek.*

ONE CANNOT FILL the void of one thing with another. *The most dangerous drugs; however, are ones that are legal and socially acceptable:*

- Human to human addiction. It makes one vulnerable to predators and love scammers.
- Addiction to toxic and fake friends, who cause harm to your life, especially when done underhandedly.
- Entertainment, especially TV and Social Media
- Shopping
- Work, especially when it leads to family neglect and serious health issues.
- Addiction to one's pain, problems, complaints and victimizing stories.
- Addictions to beliefs and ideologies.

You are what you consume, surround yourself
with, who you love, what you watch, what you
say, what you listen to, and what you choose to
be addicted to.

ADDICTION TO HUMAN BEINGS

*Prince Charming turned out to be just an accurate
description of a psychopath.*

*I know I developed an addiction to psychopaths, and dedicating a
book for it to share how I broke this addiction with the least amount of
harm possible. Psychopaths manufacture intensity and fairytales that
they know have been embedded into our daydreams thanks to Walt
Disney. No matter how much we grow and evolve, we all still have a
soft spot for those, who make us feel special, and present us with a
chance to visit our childhood wonderland.*

PSYCHOPATHS: ASCENDED MASTERS

Not all who are breathing are alive. Some die of
emotional pneumonia by the coldness of their
soulless hearts and the virus that destroyed
their conscience.

Psychopaths have zero affective empathy. They do tend to
have excellent cognitive empathy. From a psychopath's point of
view, he told me that emotions are overrated, and they are the
main obstacle to our safety and prevent us from truly seeing
through people. I was perplexed to say the least; however, I was
willing to listen. My emotions have often compromised my
intellect, including putting me in near fatal situations with
criminals just like him.

My first encounter with a criminal psychopath was some 20 years ago. At the time, I firmly believed that everyone is inherently good; should they behave badly, it only meant something bad happened to them that made them that way. How wrong I was. This belief brought me to the brink of death a few times over. I couldn't reconcile the idea that someone looks human, but with no hint of humanity, except for when he was laughing, or raging. He was an aspiring comedian, but there was nothing funny about holding a gun to my head. I did laugh; however, which is a reaction I didn't have time to analyze then. I must have been overwhelmed with the amount of unfamiliar circumstances that laughter became the only possible way to respond. We don't know how to react when we don't know what to think. Once thoughts shut down, so do their respective emotions, and reactions become random. He was in the driver's seat of my car; me in the passenger seat. Los Angeles was a new city for me. I had only been there for six months, when he introduced me to Mulholland drive and all the gruesome crimes that took place there. Sitting in the car, surrounded by darkness in a residential area on a winding road with the hills threatening more danger. It's amazing what you learn about yourself staring down the barrel of a gun. My laughter made him go nuts, as though there was more crazy in him left to reveal. He grabbed my hair so hard, I had no idea it's so firmly planted into our skulls. When he finally released me, I backed into the car door, staring at him in disbelief. In his frustration, he opened my door, pushed one of his legs against my abdomen. I flew out of the car and he sped away before I fully rested on the ground.

A nice smile isn't enough to earn you trust;
unfortunately, it often does.

With his horror stories still fresh in my mind, imagining the Hillside Stranglers, or Richard Ramirez, the Night Stalker, or someone like them coming for me, I began to pray for my psychopath to come back. He did. I got back into the car. A psychopath you know is certainly less frightening than one you don't. This is how my journey began into the world of psychopathy, and its near-fatal aftermath. Whether it is insanity or stubbornness, I had to understand, and this is why, once I escaped this man two years later, with a trail of destruction that took me 20 more years to recover from, my hunt began for more of his kind. There was no way I would have left it at that.

* * *

WHEN I CAME across Dr. Robert D. Hare, everything started to make sense. He is a CM, a Canadian psychologist, known for his research in the field of criminal psychology. He is a professor emeritus of the University of British Columbia, where his studies center on psychopathology and psychophysiology. Opposite to popular belief, Psychopathy is not a personality disorder, but a mental illness. Even though many use the term interchangeably with Sociopathy, and despite the striking similarities, there are marked differences. The most significant one is that psychopaths are born, while sociopaths are made.

* * *

THE FOLLOWING ARE some traits that sum up a psychopath by Dr. Hare, who created a psychopathy checklist using the following four scales:
   Interpersonal/Affective
   Social Deviance
   Impulsive Lifestyle
   Antisocial Behavior

. . .

HE SPECIFIED 20 criteria to look for, and based on the score, we know where on the scale the subject lands.

The higher the score the more pathological the psychopathy, with the highest score being 40. If the subject scores 30-40, they are diagnosed a psychopath, who are usually repeat offenders. Non-psychopathic criminals score on average 22-25; whereas those with no criminal history score between 0-5. Serial killer, Ted Bundy, scored 39 on the psychopathy scale. However, this scoring system needs to be solely applied by a specialized clinician. But for the sake of knowing the signs for personal safety, or for cinematic portrayals, check the list below.

THE WAY TO score your answers is by giving each of the twenty characteristics a score of 0, 1, or 2 based on how intense its relevance is to the subject:

- Glib and superficial charm
- Grandiose (exaggeratedly high) estimation of self
- Need for stimulation
- Pathological lying
- Cunning and manipulativeness
- Lack of remorse or guilt
- Shallow affect (superficial emotional responsiveness)
- Callousness and lack of empathy
- Parasitic lifestyle
- Poor behavioral controls
- Sexual promiscuity
- Early behavior problems
- Lack of realistic long-term goals
- Impulsivity
- Irresponsibility
- Failure to accept responsibility for own actions
- Many short-term marital relationships

- Juvenile delinquency
- Criminal versatility
- Revocation of conditional release (*this is when they are released from prison on a conditional basis, which they usually break; their release is revoked and a warrant for their arrest is obtained*)

Even though psychopaths are a minority, there is a high probability you have come across one. They are social predators and usually disguise themselves well as they infiltrate themselves in all areas of life. They can be easily found in high profile corporations, or stalking the night looking for someone to kill. There is a technology called, "Transcranial Magnetic Stimulation" aka TMS. It's a magnetic device that scientist attach to the head, which triggers your amygdala and the surrounding area that is responsible for Empathy and Emotions. You become a temporary psychopath, unable to feel disgust or horror at morbid images, but feel elated and struggle to keep from smirking. A good indication someone may be a psychopath is when you notice an involuntary smirk on their face when you are going through a crisis. Since they mimic others as much as they can, you may notice how they confuse reactions at times.

Nothing about him is real. The dream he sold you on is completely manufactured.

Psychopaths are the most emotionally illiterate, because they don't give much thought to emotions. Our humanity is made up of emotions, and psychopaths have a severe deficiency, which is why they feel contempt and envy due to this lack. What we deem important of our relationships, kindness, joy, and general feelings, psychopaths don't care for, because these are things they are unable to relate to or invoke in themselves. They would tell you how emotions are overrated, and how they are the cause of human weakness. They resent you for being happy and able to connect with others. Holidays and birthdays are occasions the psychopath loves to ruin. They cannot connect with what is right, good, and kind. When someone asked Ted Bundy, the serial killer, why he would think murder is bad, Bundy compared it to jay walking. To him, it is simply against the law. Ironically, he was a law student, intelligent, and used to volunteer in a suicide hotline center. Most psychopaths are not murderous freaks, who look like a boogyman. Some of them are equipped with handsomeness, charm, wit, and success. They are often found in major corporations, high political ranks, and are often doctors, surgeons, and spiritual leaders.

NOTE: *Please refrain from diagnosing the people around you. If you are in danger, it doesn't matter what diagnosis they have. Just seek appropriate help.*

* * *

PSYCHOPATHY VS. SOCIOPATHY

> What does it matter which one they are? Run, but
> quietly.

1. NATURE VS. NURTURE
Psychopaths are born, while Sociopaths are made. A sociopath is a product of society and upbringing. Many psychopaths come from loving homes.

2. CONSCIENCE
A psychopath is born without a conscience, and a sociopath

has a conscience; however, twisted. In a brain scan, the area where most people would develop a conscience, is non-existent in the psychopathic brain. It is a "birth defect," so to speak.

3. REMORSE

A psychopath has no remorse, no matter the circumstances, while a sociopath can feel remorse, if his actions went against his code of conduct. For example, a sociopath may not feel any remorse over stealing from a major corporation, but feels remorseful if he steals from a fellow thief. Remorse is something we learn by way of punishment. Whatever we were punished for as children, it becomes a behaviour that is remorse worthy. If we are raised in a permissive environment, where negative behaviour is normal, we will not feel remorse. Conflicting upbringing causes people to be repulsed by those, who are different. We adopt the ethical code instilled in us, and those, who don't uphold it, are considered, either immoral, or uptight.

4. THE MOTIVATION

What drives a psychopath is pleasure, while a sociopath is driven by personal gain. Much like the narcissist, he will remove any obstacles in his way and eradicate any person in the way of his desires. Whereas a psychopath may cause tremendous harm for no particular reason.

5. MENTAL ILLNESS VS. MOOD DISORDER:

Cluster B personalities are marked by emotional dysregulation, while Psychopaths barely have any. They are almost exclusively driven by desire, anger, fear, and boredom. It feels to me that the psychopath cannot do anything about his illness; whereas a sociopath can choose to be a better human being.

* * *

Psychopathic Indifference vs. Buddhist Detachment

Since I was 12, I have been exploring the world of Meditation, and later observed the striking resemblance between a meditative state and a psychopathic disposition. Being emotionally blunted like a psychopath is painful, while being spiritually grounded is loving and serene. They mark both ends of the emotional spectrum for the same goal, that is, the ability to observe without being influenced. When meditation became a trend, many people began to demonstrate indifference rather than detachment. There is a stark difference between not getting involved verses not giving a shit. Many friends can be lost due to this mix-up. Being detached does not mean we stop holding space for others, and offering support. The concept of self-love is often confused with selfishness. Narcissism flourished due to a misconception of the world of spirituality. Meditation isn't about sitting quietly, breathing in and out to soothing music, while letting the world burn to the ground around you. Meditation is a lifestyle and a state of being.

We embody it, while still taking care of our responsibilities, including being there for our loved ones when they need us. To love oneself means to take care of ourselves and our overall health so we can give abundantly rather than running on empty. To use meditation and spirituality as an excuse for being callous and indifferent will neither offer fulfillment, nor is it going to end well for any of us.

If I were to choose a super power, it would be to install a conscience into psychopaths.

THE DARK TRIAD

In psychology, this refers to the existence of three traits in one individual:

1. PSYCHOPATHY: a mental illness
2. Narcissism: a personality disorder
3. Machiavellianism: a personality trait of someone whose main motivation is to manipulate and exploit others for personal gain. This person sees people as a means to an end.

* * *

WRITING A PSYCHOPATH

A conversation I had with a psychopath:

> *"They say a psychopath has a god complex."*
> *"It's not a complex. I have the power to take a life".*
> *He said.*
> *"But you can't resurrect one." I fired back.*

My process began like this: When I was writing a screenplay with a psychopathic protagonist, I read all the books and resources I could find. Besides the ones I encountered in my life, there was something still missing. I used to visit an incredible hypnotherapist, Pierre-Etienne Vannier, who I credit for much of my healing. One day, I asked him to hypnotize me to delve into my protagonist's subconscious. I needed access into the part of himself he would never reveal.

Fully immersed in my research, I had two more spiritual incidents. The first one was Ted Bundy, the serial killer, visiting me in a lucid dream. It was vivid and palpable and resembling an out-of-body experience. I asked him personal questions that I couldn't find answers for in his biographies. He answered in an authentic and vulnerable manner. He confessed that he is scared.

Suddenly, it dawned on me; there is a striking resemblance between a psychopathic killer and an innocent animal looking for a prey. He was looking for connection. Murder is largely about control, but the control is motivated by a need for a specific emotion.

My second encounter was not so pleasant. I only had one more psychopathic serial killer to research, and that was Richard Ramirez, the Night Stalker. My writing was lacking something. It sounded as though I was glorifying my protagonist, just like the media, and failing to connect with his ugliness. When I started reading "The Night Stalker" I had a nightmare on the first night. Again, it was lucid, where I was being victimized by Ramirez. I woke up in tearful panic. Shortly after, I felt grateful for accessing the emotions of the victims. Even though I survived one, I still, thankfully, didn't go through what those victims did; may they rest in peace. This is how stories are balanced and unbiased when it comes to character development. It is important to empathize with both, the predator and the prey.

THE ACTOR'S PROCESS

Anthony Hopkins as Dr. Hannibal Lecter in Silence of the Lambs, and Red Dragon, Joaquin Phoenix and Heath Ledger as Joker, and Mike Emerson from LOST were impeccable in portraying a psychopath. My absolute favorite depiction was that of Mike Emerson, because we get to see his character arch throughout the seasons. What makes it most challenging for actors is that they have to break many of the acting rules, because they have to break the rules of being human. The way I would advise any actor taking on a psychopathic character is to refrain from perceiving an act of evil as evil. The brilliance is in executing a criminal act in the same manner and ease one would paint, or drink coffee. Depending on the character's motivation for murder, you will know how to best approach it. A murderer looking for connection will seem hungrier than one motivated by significance.

RAGE CAN BE cold and non-hysterical. A murderer can kill the way he paints a masterpiece. The point is to stick to the motivation and not make a big deal out of the crime itself. There is nothing worse than watching an actor trying to prove they are evil.

Psychopaths have a vicious innocence about them as a wild animal does. They don't think themselves evil. They act out of instinct like jungle animals, and are not bothered by the impact, their behaviour has on others, just like children. They, do; however, feel their own pain, and they feel fear.

EMPATHIZING WITH PSYCHOPATHS FOR OUR SAFETY

Remember, empathizing with someone does not mean we exonerate them, or allow them into our lives. Rather, we empathize to gain better understanding of them. We get to be a few steps ahead. We cannot fight, prevent, or escape what we do not understand. If you know what to look for, you have a better chance at avoiding them altogether. Empathy will serve you well when you need to know how, and when to get out of harm's way. It takes a special method to rescue yourself from a psychopath targeting you.

NOTE: *Not all psychopaths are male.*

Detectives

> Victory is challenging when your enemy has
> nothing left to lose.

Psychopaths are conniving, and manipulative. I do not buy into the popular belief that they are all intelligent; however, enough of them may be.

THEIR INTELLIGENCE IS COMPROMISED by their inability to understand emotions, or foresee consequences. It is limited to their mind games, and many of them do play the system by withholding critical information. Measuring intelligence, people forget emotional intelligence, which is pretty lacking in those types. To get a psychopath to confess to murder, a detective needs to provoke his ego and not plead to their emotions and mercy. Sometimes, it proves useful to just get out of their way.

THESE TALKERS often trip themselves up due to their overestimation of themselves and the underestimation of others. They believe they can outsmart the most seasoned detective. Fortunately for us, they're wrong.

Their low EQ marks their downfall. When reprimanded, they lash out like children.

A CLEVER DETECTIVE can be a few moves ahead, which earns him the psychopath's trust and respect. They will always trickle critical information such as where they buried the bodies, but eventually the psychopath gets pressured when his manipulations are no longer effective.

HUMAN RESOURCES

> When your job listing describes criteria for the
>   ideal candidate fits the criteria of a psychopath,
>   he will seem like an asset until your company
>   sinks into oblivion.

The last thing you need is a psychopath within your company. They often know how to climb to the top fast, earn the trust of top management, trample on anyone in their way, and by the time they get to the CEO, they have already driven the company to bankruptcy and total ruin. The psychopath embodies all the characteristics needed for business, except for honesty and integrity. They have tunnel vision focus on their goals, but not yours. Without honesty, and loyalty, any other positive traits will be meaningless.

THERAPISTS

> Like everyone else, a psychopath has a deep need
>   to be seen and heard. But he will watch you
>   closely to get under your skin.

Psychopaths don't find any fault with themselves, so going to therapy is not on their list. Unless it is court ordered, they may never see a therapist in their life.

WHEN THEY DO GO to therapy, they gain deeper insight into human behaviour and vulnerabilities, and a few more tricks to hone in their manipulation techniques. It may not be the best idea to send them to therapy, unless it's solely for scientific research. It doesn't bode well to call out a psychopath or to offer a diagnosis. There is nothing to be gained from that and everything to lose. It is best to let them talk, and keep your inferences to yourself. Otherwise, when you bring it to their attention, they will intentionally say things to prove you wrong, mind themselves as much as possible, and if they want to, they will target you personally in whatever way they see fit.

Prison Guards

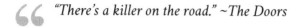 *"There's a killer on the road." ~The Doors*

The audacity it took Ted Bundy to escape twice is beyond my comprehension. Once through the courthouse window, the second from his cell in a high security prison. For his second escape, he lost a lot of weight to fit himself through the ceiling vent, crawled through the walls, and casually jumped down into the guard's apartment, took a jacket, and strolled out the door. He went on a killing spree that was so gruesome, he surpassed himself. When he was apprehended, he shared his escape story as a funny anecdote:

"There was police everywhere, and they asked civilians to join the hunt. When I encountered an old man with a rifle up in the mountains, as I was pretending to jog, I slowed down so he doesn't shoot me. He warned me about the loose serial killer. To look casual, I smiled and thanked him, then proceeded to pick flowers until he walks away. He kept staring for so long that by the time I got out of his sight, I had a genuine bouquet."

THE EMOTIONAL INNOCENCE of the psychopathic mind can generate some serious humor.

· · ·

A Romantic Partner

He will charm his way into your heart, and then
try to eat it.

There will be a one-sided agreement. You will do as he says, or he will destroy you and your family. This man will manufacture intensity to get you hooked, and will keep everything you hold dear hostage. If you think you can so much as eat without his permission, there will be grave consequences. Should you choose to stay, know you will have to leave your basic human rights at the door, and your future will be in his hands. You will look in the mirror and you won't find your soul. He takes it away too. And always remember, they respond to kindness, humor and, at times, retreat when you mirror back their violent outbursts, than they ever would to niceness, pleading and visible fear. They are cowards, and sometimes you will have go psycho on them. Don't try that though.

Empathy Check Point

The only time he ever apologized was to the first
person he had killed; himself.

The first murder victim is always the one pulling the trigger. Always. You cannot murder anyone with such pleasure, unless you're dead inside. This is what it feels like to be a psychopath. Whether they commit murder or not, a psychopath is plagued by emptiness and boredom. They often gravitate towards persons with an abundant variety of emotions.

THERE IS unspoken mutual benefit to this duo. We often wish to take a much needed break from our emotions, and enjoy the company of a psychopath, and they get to experience human life through our presence.

THERE IS nothing to be envious of when it comes to psychopaths. The inability to feel a variety of emotions, is a painful existence. The void in the soul is palpable. We experience emotions in technicolor, while psychopaths experience four dull, shallow emotions at best, and often, not even simultaneously.

We are all capable of being callous when we perceive a threat to our loved ones, and our most pressing needs. It is not the same as being born without a conscience, but due to our intense moments of self-absorption and when our survival is on the line, we can become incapable of empathy; we can act in cold-hearted ways when tested and when our threshold is reached.

Thoughtlessness can make temporary psychopaths
of us.

It's a temporary loss of conscience. Extreme desperation will shut down our conscience pretty fast. We all can become evil. What sets us apart is our intention, our choices, and our thresholds. The simplest way to embody a psychopath is, first, by not thinking of them as such. See them as innocent children, or animals in the wild with the sole concern for survival.

An animal can surely be vicious when hunting, and looks frightening as it devours its prey, but they have an innocence about them, because they don't see it as an act of violence. The animal is simply surviving and being present in the moment. This is how the psychopath lives.

. . .

MYTHS ABOUT PSYCHOPATHS

1. HIGH I.Q: Some are and some aren't. They are not necessarily intelligent, or intellectual. No matter how conniving they are, evil is never a quality of the smart.

2. THEY ARE all murderers and criminals: Most psychopaths don't commit murder. Many occupy high places. They are not stalled by emotions, which has been a requirement for success. They are willing to step over anyone, and be cold-hearted in the name of business and country.

3. THEY ARE PSYCHOTIC: Psychosis is the inability to differentiate between what is real and what is not. Psychopaths know exactly what they are doing. They are pragmatic thinkers. However, they cannot grasp the concept of right and wrong. You may think to yourself that a person must be crazy to cause this much harm. In layman's terms, sure, we can call them crazy.

IN THE EYES of the law, they are not. This is why they go to prison rather than a mental institution. There is no fixing for them. Unless they invent a way to install a conscience, psychopaths will remain the same and will remain repeat-offenders. It is their nature.

Morally, they are irrevocably corrupt. Most of them do not commit murder, but they are all cunning, calculating and narcissistic, leaving a trail of destruction behind.

* * *

Divorcing a Psychopath

> "Why didn't you just grant her the divorce? Why
> couldn't you find anything else to do besides
> murder? Why didn't you let her live?" I asked.
> He smirked and said: "Because murder binds us
> together. I love her. Divorcing her means I let
> her go. And I can't let that bitch go."

*IF YOU HAVE the misfortune of dating or marrying one, then make sure
to exit the relationship safely. The general rules don't apply here.*

HOW TO ESCAPE SAFELY:

1. Comply to them and avoid confrontations as much as possible. Be loving and clingy. Nagging can sometimes work for them to leave you alone. Ask for the complete opposite of what you want. Only you know what works best with your partner.

2. Secretly, plan your new life. Do not share your intentions with him, or anyone. People may snitch, and often babble mindlessly. You cannot casually ask for a divorce.

3. Save money in a secret account. You cannot risk having receipts or letters in your shared mail. You can always get a mailbox at the post-office and make sure they never forward you anything. You can always go pick it up, read it, then store it back.

4. If you have children, make sure they are financially covered. If this is not possible, then apply for financial aid. They will use the children to make your life a living hell, and will turn them against you. That is, if you are still allowed to see them.

5. Record any abuse as much as possible without getting caught. If there is any physical evidence of abuse, take pictures

of all bruises, and keep a journal. Store them in a safety deposit box at the bank.

6. Have a solid support network, but do not involve too many people. Choose them wisely. They have to be trustworthy, and useful to the situation. If they cannot help you, they don't need to know. Psychopaths are insightful when it comes to reading people and sensing fear. You don't want an awkward facial expression to blow your cover.

7. Let the authorities know of your escape plan. They may assist you. Be sure you are not seen or followed. Best do so using a payphone. You can ask a female cop to meet you at a supermarket out of uniform.

8. Make sure when you check out resources for victims of domestic violence, you do not do so on your computer that the psychopath has access too. Often, they install spyware and even track your car. Make any calls that your partner may find suspicious using a payphone.

9. Remain calm, and do not rush the process.

10. Do not disclose your new location and block them on all social media. Better yet, do not share anything on social media. Close your account.

NOTE: *When you have a psychopath in your life, do not ever believe they're gone, even after you leave. They tend to come back, stalk and obsess over their past partners despite their prolonged silences and disappearances. Don't let that fool you. They do not like to lose. While you can always file for a protective order, it doesn't necessarily protect you. You need to take extra safety measures. Keep your doors and windows locked, and have a security camera installed. Sometimes, unfortunately, people have to leave town altogether and start over elsewhere.*

* * *

Lessons of a Psychopath

In the beginning, dealing with psychopaths was especially frustrating, given we landed on the opposite ends of the emotional sensitivity scale. They would accuse me of being too emotional, and I would call them tin men. As time went on, and as I was growing tired of feeling too much, getting my heart broken repeatedly, and not knowing how to process the intensity and ups and downs, I started to listen a bit more intently. I figured, maybe they have a point there. At a painful time in my life, I googled how to be a psychopath in terms of not feeling heartbroken anymore. It was a useless endeavor. Canceling pain meant canceling joy just the same, and I couldn't cancel anything anyway. Still, I was willing to learn the lessons I needed just enough to balance my thoughts and emotions a bit better. *Here are some valuable lessons they offered:*

- Keep it simple.
- Don't believe what you think. You think you love someone, but you don't. Stop confusing infatuation with love.
- Why are you infatuated by someone, who is nothing like the image you created of him? Let's break it down.
- When you are heartbroken, what are you thinking? That you will never find anyone else? Because it's not true.
- If someone is a jerk to you, why would you think highly of them? You think they will magically change?
- You're in love with an idea.
- The way you look at things are creating the emotions. Adjust your thoughts.
- Go be alone for a while. Sort yourself out before you even think of dating.
- Last time you were heartbroken, you felt the same

way. Don't you think these emotions are coming from you and have nothing to do with him?

- When you first meet someone, let them show you who they are before you share anything with them. Why do you always have to tell someone what your triggers or boundaries are? You just exposed your vulnerabilities for him to take advantage of.
- Just because someone looks nice doesn't mean they are good.
- People will always try to get away with something no matter how good you are. Don't be the one giving them the pass.
- No one needs to know your inner world.
- Observe before you trust.
- Stop assigning people good qualities they haven't yet proven. Look for the pattern. Patterns take time.
- Since you fall in love easily with what people show you in the beginning, then you need some distance.
- Your vulnerability gets you in trouble. It is fine to be vulnerable as long as you don't show it to those you don't know.
- Focus on yourself and what you want. If someone fits in your plan then great. If they don't, don't jump off your path and join them on theirs. This is why you get devastated. It's insane.
- Know your worth so you don't believe those, who try to minimize you.
- If they're not good for you, then good riddance.

Thanks to the lessons, I kept it all simple and summed it up in a sentence I use as a mantra:

Anything that can be lost is never a loss.

Psychopaths as Ascended Masters

One evening, I was deep in contemplation about the purpose of psychopaths. I was feeling emotionally and mentally spent, trying to make sense of the demon I got involved with. I heard a voice within, reminding me that all things are lessons. I wondered if evil people in general are actually ascended masters, who volunteered to play this challenging role for the sake of helping us evolve and learn our lessons.

A sense of comfort washed over me as I basked in the positive possibilities of my new-found perspective. Looking for the lessons somehow empowered me. I saw him as a teacher, here to serve my highest good. If it wasn't for the worst among us, we would have never learned the lessons we needed for our spiritual development. Once the lesson is received, the universe clears our path from the dark forces that were blocking the light of our wisdom. The most valuable lessons we digest are the ones we receive during the toughest trials. The worst among us are those, who challenge us the most, and are also those we learn the most from about ourselves and about the world.

Rarely, do the lessons of our loved ones stick, if not enhanced by personal experience. The darker the forces, the brighter the light that follows. It is empowering to claim the gems among the rubble. This is how beget to own our stories, and rise from the ashes created by monsters in human form. Refuse to be victimized by the experience.

PERSONALITY DISORDERS

> No one can devalue what is deemed valuable by
> the divine. It is useless to idealize that which is
> not, in essence, ideal.

There are three clusters of Personality Disorders according to the DSM (Diagnostic and Statistical Manual of Mental Disorders). Cluster A, The Eccentric types, Cluster B, the Dramatic types and Cluster C, the Anxious/Fearful types.

I am only going to focus on Cluster B, the Dramatic Types, who I refer to as *"Sensational Victims".* I believe these personalities are some of the most challenging to deal with, and the least understood because their illness is largely caused by emotional dysregulation and inconsistency.

USING a disorder as a derogatory term is not helpful, and shouldn't be acceptable. It is a real illness. Making an effort to understand Cluster B personalities may save you from the trail of destruction they tend to leave behind. Tormented souls don't know any other way. When they do get together, they wreak havoc on themselves and each other. I always felt society tends to mirror these four types, especially under oppressive regimes.

THE FOUR CORNERSTONES of life can be divided by these four categories:
   1. *Money—————> Antisocial Personality.*
   2. *Ideology—————>Narcissistic Personality.*
   3. *Politics—————>Histrionic Personality.*
   4. *Relationship——>Borderline Personality.*

. . .

Cluster B: The Dramatic Types

> When emotional immaturity is coupled with
> biological maturity, it is a clear sign of a
> pathology.

Antisocial Personality Disorder: The Sociopath

> If you want to know someone's deepest fears and
> insecurities, observe the methods they use to
> punish you.

Antisocial Personality Disorder (Sociopathy) shares many of the criteria for Psychopathy. The differences are listed under Psychopathy in the previous chapter. Since a sociopath is a product of upbringing, we have to look at the environment they grew up in. Raising the collective awareness of the serious repercussions of sociopathy is detrimental to society at large. Not all communities, who breed sociopaths, are inherently indifferent.

While poverty can be a catalyst, so is extreme wealth. The only difference is in the manner they demonstrate the behavior. Boredom can make some people sink into dark thoughts. The thoughts we feed accentuate and it is only a matter of time before we act on them. Family annihilators such as Scott Peterson and Chris Watts are horrifying examples of that. One of the most terrifying crimes was the murder of 16-year-old Skylar Neese by multiple stabbings. The killers were her two, gorgeous-looking, best friends. Her childhood friend, Sheila Eddy, is a psychopath, and their third friend, Rachel Shoaf, is a sociopathic narcissist.

· · ·

EXCESSIVE COCAINE USE can lead to sociopathic behavior. I don't believe a drug or a community can be fully to blame, because not everyone will become sociopathic under these circumstances. Pressure, power and certain drugs reveal what's already inside. Of course, some drugs can force you far off out of your character, such as date-rape drugs. Prolonged use of some drugs will alter your brain, shut down your emotional sensors, and alter your personality. However, we cannot use external agents as a crutch to justify our own choices.

EMPATHY LEVELS IN ANTISOCIAL PERSONALITIES:

They have healthy **cognitive empathy**, which is called Cold Empathy. They are usually particularly good at empathizing with concepts and intellectual views that are devoid of emotions. It is as though they have an x-ray vision into people's character. They sniff out fears and vulnerabilities as predators often do.

They have low to non-existent **affective empathy**. They do not empathize with others' emotions and moods.

Affective definition: denoting or relating to mental/personality disorders in which disturbance of mood is the primary symptom.

EMPATHY CHECK POINT:

Their upbringing normalized or encouraged sociopathic behavior. Sometimes, we may perceive a person to be sociopathic, because we perceive the behavior to be negative. One community's idol is another community's sociopath. However, when it comes to murder, it is often traced back to upbringing, parental neglect and betrayal. Manipulation may be the only method they know to get what they want. Some people make a conscious decision to become sociopathic, because they were badly harmed for being kind. Society encourages us to compartmentalize our emotions. We cannot suppress one emotion without suppressing its opposite. Sociopaths suppress their remorse and ignore their conscience. Many sociopathic behaviors are becoming normalized now, and we are collectively responsible for that.

* * *

2. NARCISSISTIC PERSONALITY DISORDER: THE TIN MAN

> I thought it is understood that you are my prey.
> You don't get to have a say.

Many people think of excessive self-love when they think of Narcissism, but, in truth, they are driven by deep-seated self-loathing. They spend their lives masking it with arrogance, self-obsession, and self-adulation. They idealize and devalue themselves just as they do unto others. It is rather an unrequited self-love doomed by self-rejection. The only way to numb this painful reality is by way of projection.

CRITERIA ACCORDING TO THE DSM:
PLEASE NOTE THAT THE CRITERIAL IN THE DSM FOCUS ON THE OVERT TYPE OF NARCISSISTS AND NOT THE COVERT

- Has an inflated/grandiose sense of self-importance
- Is preoccupied with fantasies of success, power, brilliance, beauty, or ideal love
- Believes that he or she is "special" and can only be understood by other special or high-status people
- Requires excessive admiration
- Possesses a sense of entitlement

- Takes advantage of others
- Lacks Empathy
- Envious of others or believes others are envious of him/her
- Behaves in an arrogant, egotistical, or haughty way
- Exploitative and manipulative
- Mostly emotionally and mentally abusive, but physical, financial, sexual, or spiritual abuse is not beyond them.
- They engineer and feed off drama
- Triangulates
- Gaslights
- Never gives credit unless for personal gain
- Lack of responsibility and accountability

* * *

TYPES OF NARCISSISTS

Narcissism is a wide spectrum that ranges from a few mild traits to a full-fledged disorder. Most are closet bisexuals. If their orientation causes them deep shame, they deflect it through abusing others. They tend to have a marked disdain for women, and use them as beards, and to exert control.

- ### MALIGNANT NARCISSIST

THIS TYPE of narcissist is the most malicious, and closely resembles sociopaths and psychopaths. They tend to be overt, but they can also be maliciously covert. Other narcissists may cause harm out of necessity, but malignant narcissists would cause harm for their own amusement.

• OVERT NARCISSIST: THE GRANDIOSE TYPE

THIS TYPE IS OUTSPOKEN, visibly grandiose, overtly aggressive, directly nasty and disrespectful, and has no qualms about clearly expressing their self-admiration. They are often flamboyant, loud, and in love with the spotlight. They are overtly shameless, despite their deep-seated shame. Overcompensation is in full drive with the overt type. When they are female, they are often diagnosed with Histrionic personality disorder; however, despite the similarities, some differences set them apart.

THINGS THEY MIGHT SAY:

- *Look at my beauty. Have you seen anyone this gorgeous?*
- *Everyone thinks you are crazy. You're not very smart are you?*
- *I am way smarter than you can ever be.*
- *You have a wild imagination. None of this ever happened.*
- *I never said this. I have never done that! (this can be said while they are doing the thing they're denying)*
- *I am the best at this. They're just envious of me.*
- *Your apology is not enough. You have to drop to your knees, kiss my hand, and ask for forgiveness.*

• COVERT NARCISSIST: THE INVERTED/THE VULNERABLE

This is the most dangerous kind because they know how to cover their tracks, and no one sees their abuse but you. This one is passive-aggressive and is much more frustrating to deal with than the overt narcissists. They use the silent treatment, stonewalling, manipulation, but will make sure there is nothing you can hold against them. Those around you will think you are the abusive one, while they are too kind to leave you. Some people call this type the Vulnerable Narcissist; I call them snakes and hyenas based on the way they operate.

THINGS THEY MIGHT SAY:

- *I am such a loser. Oh, I just like to keep myself humble so all this admiration I get from everyone doesn't get to my head.*
- *Oh my god, I have to do everything myself to save the day.*
- *I feel bad for my friend. His girlfriend keeps flirting with me, and I don't know what to do about it.*
- *Everyone thinks I look like (insert name of a really good looking celebrity)*
- *I'm fine, don't worry about it. (followed by sulking)*
- *I'm sorry you feel that way/Sorry, you feel hurt.*
- *You shouldn't feel this way. You should be glad.*
- *It's ok, you're uptight.*
- *Oh, wow! And I thought my ex was crazy.*
- *I'm pretty sure everyone else treats you like shit.*
- *Silence.*

Covert Narcissists want to get a rise out of you, so the best thing to do is not get defensive. Better yet, get them out of your life. If you have to deal with one, keep it superficial and love them from a distance.

- ### CEREBRAL NARCISSIST: THE ASEXUAL

The cerebral type is concerned with his intellect rather than his physical desires. They collect medals, certificates, and accomplishments, or simply fake them. They may be talkers, but not doers. They brag about their sexual conquests, when, in truth, they barely have a sex life. Many of them are asexual. They will only engage in sex to influence and control, but once they reach their end goal, they will be repulsed by any show of intimacy and will withhold it from their partner. To them, physical intimacy is used as a weapon, a tactic, or a bargaining chip, when they have to. They may get married and have children as a cover.

A cerebral narcissist spent a decade posing as a surgeon and worked in high profile hospitals. Many patients would die under his knife. Hospitals would let him go quietly, because they wanted to avoid lawsuits, and neglected to warn other hospitals. By the time he was caught, he had a lot of blood on his hands. When asked how he pulled it off for so long, he said, "I read a lot."

• SOMATIC NARCISSIST: THE DIVA

This one is often preoccupied with sex, and it is their end goal. They use people and feel entitled to their bodies. They translate any form of attention as an invitation for sex. They believe everyone desires them, including those, who are not interested. Those, who reject them, will be lied about, and they will play games to prove to others that they are being chased by them. They manufacture situations to prove the other person's obsession with them. These are the types obsessed with their muscles; you see them flexing, working out, consuming muscle enhancing products, flaunt their cleavage, wearing revealing clothes, and seducing anyone in their path without discrimination.

NOTE: *Each type of Narcissist will behave like the other types sometimes. Once you expose a covert narcissist, they will become overt with their abuse towards you, but continue to hide it in public.*

Narcissistic Supply

> There was no negotiation with him. How dare you
> think you'd be anything more than a sounding
> board, a punching bag, and a beautifying
> mirror for his reflection?

All narcissistic relationships are a means of getting narcissistic supply. Whether they want your attention, money, body, resources, or social status, it is all about what they can get, and for how long they can get it without having to reciprocate. Narcissists will only do favors when it is in their best interest and will make seemingly faithful friends to those in high places to solidify their place with them for personal gain. This is the main reason it can take a long time before someone believes your horror stories about him because they have the most powerful already in their pocket.

Flying Monkeys

Flying monkeys are people narcissists use to build an army of abuse so to speak. These are the ones, who are either loyal to the narcissist, or unsuspecting people, who have no idea they are being used. They help the narcissist abuse you by proxy, and they also help with the smear campaign he will launch against you. Never trust any of the narcissist's flying monkeys, because you won't know who is reporting back to your abuser, and who is pretending to be your friend to get information.

Into the FOG: Fear. Obligation. Guilt.

Narcissists of every type create a mind fog by instilling fear, drowning you in obligations, and endless guilt trips. They cause much confusion and keep you too exhausted to understand what they're doing to you. No matter how openly hostile a narcissist is, you will still have a hard time winning an argument or be able to hold them accountable for anything. Evidence doesn't mean anything to them.

HERE ARE some ways they create FOG:

- The dead stare: done deliberately to scare you and usually comes out of nowhere. So you're not sure what you did wrong so you just stop doing everything.
- They will rush you to do them an urgent favor, will speak really fast to create anxiety in you, and don't give you space to think, much less say no.
- Their emergency becomes your emergency.
- If you do manage to say no, the guilt will be laid on you thick. Whether it's by stonewalling you, giving you the silent treatment, excluding you from something important to you, or simply failing to do anything that you were relying on them for.
- They use severe punishments that rarely fit the crime, which is not a crime at all. Maybe you declined to get physical too soon, couldn't help them with something minor, and they will make sure to let you think you can rely on them for a serious emergency, and they bail on you in the last second. This includes serious health hazards.

Warning: Narcissists are known to drive someone completely out of their wits to the point of pushing them to suicide, and when the victim does actually attempt it, the narcissist leaves the premises knowing there is a high chance the victim would die.

. . .

WHAT WE CAN LEARN FROM NARCISSISTS

> In everyone, there is a teacher. When you extract
> the lessons from the worst among us, then it
> wasn't a total waste.

- They teach us to love ourselves.
- They remind us of who we don't wish to become.
- We often find our self worth at the bottom of abuse.
- They remind us of our own power. They don't gravitate towards the weak.
- They let us know what makes us great by what they try to destroy.
- We learn how ugly selfishness truly is.
- We learn to appreciate good people.

MIRROR NEURONS: BIOLOGICAL EMPATHY

The human brain has mirror neurons. These neurons reflect the extent one feels an emotion for another. They replicate your emotions towards someone else and reflect them back to you. So, if you feel scorn, hatred, or disdain towards someone, you will feel those towards yourself just the same. If you observe someone else's emotion towards another, you will create the same emotion just as much. Our bodies produce the neurochemical states of mind inside us. It's impossible for a human being to seek to intentionally hurt another without hurting themselves. Furthermore, we cannot observe something without being impacted by it. As mentioned earlier in the book, the observed changes from one observer to another, but the observer is impacted by the observed just the same. A mirror neuron is a neuron that fires in the one, who acts and the one, who observes the action. The neuron "mirrors" the behavior that we observe in another, as though the observer is the one acting.

THE BROKEN MIRRORS OF NARCISSISM

A narcissist's eternal hostility can be largely due to them inflicting pain upon others consistently, and, as a byproduct, upon themselves. Splitting is a constant state for them, and so, their mirror is equally fragmented.

EMPATHY CHECK POINT:

The Narcissist is plagued with a perpetual lack of fulfillment. They may experience some happiness, but they are always dependent on external things for validation. Without others' affirmations and applause, they feel nonexistent. Their internal world dominated by doom and gloom. They are the third degree burn victims, suffering arrested development, forever feeling unheard and unacknowledged.

IT'S CHALLENGING to empathize with these human hyenas, but we can relate to their pain. A personality disorder is not an excuse to cause harm, and no one needs to tolerate it. Still, empathy can help us understand what we are dealing with, and which healthy boundaries we need to set. Narcissists have no respect for boundaries, which is why you need to learn how to apply them when dealing with them. We must collectively put an end to glorifying nasty behaviors, and find new ways to discourage Narcissists from causing harm by implementing firm consequences. Much like children, they will continue to cause harm when left to their own devices. The more society feeds their ego, the bolder they become. They feed off attention, even if negative. To them, negative supply is far better than being ignored.

* * *

3. Histrionic Personality Disorder: The Seductress

She couldn't laugh or cry or seduce you with
enough hysterics to feel worthy of your
attention. This woman wanted your soul and
then some. Once you prove your adoration, she
will be free to move on to the next admirer. But
she is perpetually unsatisfied.

DSM Criteria:

- Discomfort in situations in which you're not the center of attention
- Interaction with others that's often characterized by inappropriate sexually seductive or provocative behavior
- Rapidly shifting and shallow expression of emotion
- Consistently uses physical appearance to draw attention to self
- Style of speech that is excessively impressionistic and lacking in detail
- Shows self-dramatization, theatricality, and exaggerated expression of emotion
- Is easily influenced by others or by circumstances.
- Considers relationships to be more intimate than they actually are.

Empathy Check Point:

Inauthenticity is always a warning for impending
betrayal.

Histrionic personalities are the toughest personality types
for me to empathize with. Although a pure histrionic can be

harmless, as long as you don't introduce them to your love interest, there is something quite annoying about the fake high pitched voice, and the embellishment of false praise. They kind of force you to become fake yourself because if you don't entertain them, they will become explosive and dramatic over nothing.

They don't care about causing a scene; they seek it out as they are consistently starved for drama. If a histrionic barely knows you, don't be surprised when they run towards you with excitement, hug you and kiss you and tell you how much they love and miss you. You must reciprocate their intensity if you want to avoid starring in an embarrassing street theatre. If they decide to just shake your hand, and you miss it, because you were leaning for a kiss hello, they will explode just the same if they had their mind set to fight you anyway that day. Most of us cannot stomach hypocrisy especially when it comes in large doses. This personality loves stealing other people's romantic partner right before their eyes. They have no shame or remorse. They feel entitled to your partner, and may fight you, if you don't end your relationship.

Deep inside, Histrionic Personalities feel worthless, unlovable, and that nothing about them is enough. They are either too fat, too skinny, too much of anything negative, or too little of something positive. If you see them as children, they were the forgotten, the ignored, and those, who had to consistently be pre-occupied with what a parent was going through rather than being a child. Sometimes feelings of neglect manifest themselves through creating drama to get attention, be it through rage, loud, fake laughter, or hysterical temper tantrums.

Seduction is their main modus operandi when they grow up. They can easily trigger our inherent insecurities in fear of losing our partner to one of those sirens. This is why it's important to begin the empathy process at childhood before they became everything we resent and fear.

WE, too, can understand, what it feels like to be ignored. The histrionic ones were cheated out of their childhood. Maybe they had to grow in the shadow of a prettier sister or had to take care of a parent, who was sick, or worse, an addict. Being orphaned early in life can be another root cause, as well as being one of many children, and so they had to get loud. Haven't we all thrown a tantrum sometime?

IT TOOK me a long time to find ways to empathize with histrionics. While I was able to look at them objectively, I run the other way when I see one. There is no peace to be had here.

* * *

4. BORDERLINE PERSONALITY DISORDER: THE HEARTBROKEN

> Me? Heartbroken? Of course, I am! Can't you see
> I'm beaming with light?

This personality type is the least harmful among the Cluster B, unless there is a co-morbidity with sociopathy or malignant narcissism. Movies have slaughtered the image of those suffering Borderline Personality, and even though they tend to seek therapy, it took a long time before therapists became comfortable accepting them as patients.

They were often misdiagnosed with Bipolar Disorder, which is a mental illness, as they used to be considered the same disease. Some people with Complex Post-Traumatic Stress Disorder are misdiagnosed as Borderline Personalities.

There are 9 criteria of BPD; one has to meet at least 5 to be diagnosed as such.

- Frantic efforts to avoid real or imagined abandonment
- Unstable and intense interpersonal relationships.
- Lack of clear sense of identity.
- Impulsiveness in potentially self-damaging behaviors, such as substance abuse, sex, shoplifting, reckless driving, binge eating.
- Recurrent suicidal threats or gestures, or self-mutilating behaviors.
- Severe mood shifts and extreme reactivity to situational stresses
- Chronic feelings of emptiness.
- Frequent and inappropriate displays of anger.
- Transient, stress-related feelings of unreality or paranoia.

My biggest fear was to die of a broken heart until I realized how much more painful it is to live with one.

REASONS THEY SELF-HARM

"Enough hurting yourself my love."
"I just wanted a scar for happiness."
"Happiness doesn't have a scar."

Physical self-harm is a way to minimize internal pain. The deeper the emotional pain, the more tolerant we become of physical pain. You can measure someone's depth of emotional scarring by their physical tolerance to pain. Think of a time of great inner turmoil that caused your tolerance for physical pain to rise. When we are heartbroken, we care less about bumping into a table. But if we are happy or emotionally stable, we can get pretty dramatic when we bump into an object. This is not the same as not feeling pain during severe car accidents, because in that case, it is numbed by the rush of adrenalin.

NOTE: *Sufferers of BPD, who are not sociopathic, direct their harm mainly against themselves rather than on others. When and if they do, it is not done with malicious intent, but out of the intense fear of perceived abandonment.*

EMPATHY CHECK POINT:

Fear of abandonment is heart-wrenching. When those, they rely on most are unreliable, they are haunted by a perpetual sense of feeling unsafe. They feel tortured by their inability to trust anyone because they are unable to trust themselves. They are stuck in an infant emotional age, who are not equipped to take care of themselves emotionally. Their core wounds overpower their current reality. They are reactive to any faint threat of abandonment.

BEING HEARTBROKEN as a Borderline Personality is much more intensified than it is experienced by an emotionally balanced person. Suicide is the immediate urge to end the pain. Thanks to the rapidly shifting moods of the borderline, they often don't linger in a thought long enough to execute it. Many still, unfortunately, kill themselves. The core of their pain is abandonment, which they often bring upon themselves by obsessing about it.

They push away those they need most and attract those, they least deserve. Playing small may minimize the risk of being abandoned, they think. Whether the primary caretaker of the child has died early in the child's life, was sick and couldn't take care of the kids, decided to leave, or neglected the child altogether, the child is left vulnerable and unsafe. BPD was often mistaken for Schizophrenia, which was falsely defined as split personalities. Caretakers may laugh off the child's moodiness as they swing from crying to heartily laughing and back. They don't realize that the child is reacting to others' treatment of them. A neglected child feels somber and lonely, but find their joy quickly once their caretakers pay them kind attention. They are highly attuned to other people's thoughts and energies, and despite someone's physical presence, they can still be emotionally neglected, bullied and ridiculed. These individuals are sadly walking targets. Abandoned by parents, physically abused by a sibling, bullied at school, and raped during their formative years are a lot to bear for a child under the age of 8.

MANY BORDERLINE PERSONALITIES have experienced several forms of abuse in childhood, and were exposed to more throughout their life.

High-functioning Borderline personalities are able to achieve professional success, yet have an underlying feeling of being inadequate. They build walls around them to prevent others from seeing their vulnerability. No matter how professionally successful they are, heartbreak brings them to their knees. Borderlines are the only ones among the cluster B personalities, who can get better with time. Some say, the symptoms begin to fade by their mid-thirties, and keep getting better onwards. They are responsive to treatment and guidance. Many of the symptoms become less severe as they grow up.

Shamanic medicine has proven useful for those with BPD, because it offers them a true meaning of love and forgiveness. If any of the other disorders are present with BPD, then the healing methods may not work.

THE OTHER THREE cluster B disorders are not renowned for their ability to change. There are no cures reported to date. Like the other disorders, BPD is a mood disorder, marked by intense emotional dysregulation. They can rapidly fluctuate between two opposing emotions, which is why they cannot see themselves or others with a steady perception.

Splitting is their involuntary modus operandi. They can hurt others by idealization or devaluation. They cannot reconcile both sides of one human being. They are either all good or all bad, which changes from one day or even hour to the next. They see themselves as heroes or villains. On a good day, they feel capable of anything, then the next, they can feel gloomy, worthless, and incapacitated.

* * *

WHAT THEY ALL SHARE

1. The same wound: Parental betrayal by abandonment, enmeshment, and a lack of consistent love.
2. Emotional Dysregulation
3. Object Constancy Disturbance
4. Splitting
5. Lack of Boundaries

WHAT IS SPLITTING?

Splitting is black and white thinking. It is the inability to integrate a good side of someone with their bad side. Someone is either all good or all bad, depending on the moment. They split people and themselves in half; good Jack/Jane cannot have mistakes. Bad Jack/Jane cannot have positive traits. So, if at the moment they become disappointed with you, they will demonize all of you, and delete all of your past goodness. When they want to reconcile with you, they will assign you an idealized version of your goodness, and delete the bad. This sets you up for failure because no one is perfect or demonic all the time. The world of duality is highly accentuated for them.

> If duality is transcended, we understand that both
> sides of the coin are still the same coin.

Many people, who do not fit the criteria of personality disorders experience splitting. We fragment when we are split. When we integrate ourselves, we will be able to see ourselves and others in one piece as opposed to one piece at a time. Most conflicts resolve when we no longer go through automatic splitting.

NOTE: *Depersonalization and derealisation co-occur.*

EXAMPLES of black and white thinking:

1. My efforts are either a great success or they are an utter failure
2. Other people are either all good or all bad.
3. I am either all good or all bad.
4. If you're not with us, you're against us

And the pendulum never rests.

CHAPTER 6
THE CRIMINAL ABYSS
EMPATHY SCARCITY

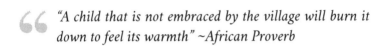 *"A child that is not embraced by the village will burn it down to feel its warmth" ~African Proverb*

We have been witnessing a staggering rise in emotional abuse, and there is a reason for that. We no longer live in an actual jungle, yet we never stepped out of survival mode. Mentally, we are still there. There is no outlet for the intense adrenalin rushes, fears, and frustrations. Physically attacking each other comes at a high price. This is especially true in big cities, places of work, and schools. It is now regarded as unacceptable behavior that is punishable by law and by society alike. With no outlet for our frustrations, people resort to emotional abuse. Many are suppressed to such a degree that they, either, implode or explode. When they finally do, it is gruesome.

Emotional abuse turns many, otherwise regular people, into murderers. Whether it's a bullied student, who snapped, and sets out to kill his entire class, or a regular husband, who wakes up one day to kill his wife and children, we need to stop and reconsider the way we pressure each other out of our wits.

. . .

THE LACK of empathy in criminals is often met with an equal lack of empathy by the average person. Social media has revealed to all of us the kind of darkness humans are capable of. If emotional abuse continues to be ignored, crime will become the norm. We are already half way there. We need to take cases like these as a solemn warning to where we are headed at this time.

It is worth noting that emotional abuse does not have to turn physical for it to be considered serious. It causes fatal illnesses, destruction to personal lives, and pushes many to suicide.

CRIMES OF APATHY

> If I were to pray for protection from evil, it would
> be that of the humankind. Should humans be
> kind, all else will be bearable.

All crimes are crimes of ignorance under Divine Law. Then again, not all crimes, under the law of man are, in fact, crimes at all. These are crimes of subtle dehumanization. Murderers used to say they'd rather not be privy to personal information about their victims, so they don't perceive them as human. It makes it easier for them to torture someone, if they are not getting personal in that sense. But crime is personal and has extremely personal repercussions. It is no longer limited to career criminals. It infiltrated the hearts of our wives, husbands, siblings, parents, and children.

The average person often divests another to be able to continue causing them harm. They refuse to acknowledge anything positively humane about their target of devaluation. It may seem harmless, but it's not. I believe it's much more damaging, because it is common, socially acceptable, and often celebrated. The victim is alive through it. When we depersonalize everything, we end up dehumanizing each other.

Crimes such as homicide, rape, false imprisonment, and human trafficking get most of the attention and rightfully so. However, we need to look at those unnoticeable little things that propel those crimes. Our basic need is to connect and belong. To belong, we need to know we are accepted, seen and heard. Shame is a dehumanizing agent, and this is by far the most dangerous weapon of all. You may be shamed into going to war, shamed into silence if you were raped, shamed for being unique, or shamed for being a survivor of a crime. We are continuously shamed for being human, and are shamed for showing emotion and empathy. Dehumanization is the root of every crime against others and against the self. It is the utter degradation of the human spirit.

> There are a few things I can think of that are far
> worse than death.

MODERN DAY DEHUMANIZATION

> Be careful stripping people of their dignity, and
> their humanity; you won't know how to reason
> with them when they come for you.

1. *INDIFFERENCE*

> We may not be able to shut down the circus, but
> we can stop contributing to it.

The quote *"Not my circus, not my monkeys"* sounds like a funny quote, and while it may sound true to you, it is not. We live in an interconnected Universe on a cellular level that is also timeless. We need to realize that statements like these are the core issue for racism, sexism, apartheid, injustice, and sociopathy.

This is our circus, and yes, these are our monkeys, because we are the monkeys and the circus. If you behave like a sociopath and inspire others to do the same, you will have to eventually face the very monsters you helped create. If something makes you uncomfortable, such as a grieving friend, a loved one going through a challenge, or someone, who needs you for moral support, then remember that your comfort is a privilege and not the primary concern when something more pressing is asking for your time and attention. There are priorities. Or you can choose to disappear on people when they need you, only to wake up one day, and find yourself alone. The retaliation of those subjected to consistent injustice is a real and near threat to the original perpetrators. They will burn the circus to the ground without mercy or discrimination.

* * *

2. Character Assassination aka Bloodless Murder

> Do not hold people hostage to your ideas. You are
> causing more damage than you know. Had you
> only known, you would forever hold your
> peace.

Committing character assassination and slander leaves you with nothing superior but the cold blood spatter on your hands. Getting murdered symbolically is a lot worse than physical death. You get to experience it consistently. Murder weapons aren't always guns, knives, or poison. They can be cutting comments, toxic silence, exclusion, scorn, and mass acts of psychic and energetic violence. Most murderers are running free among us. Even religions expressed how shunning and discord are graver than committing physical murder.

IMPACT OF CHARACTER ASSASSINATION:

- Complex Post Traumatic Stress Disorder.
- Loss of income. Inability to afford food, medication, doctors, rent, and utilities.
- An endangerment of one's life through direct, and indirect threats.
- Frequent public humiliation, and re-traumatization.
- Inability to defend oneself, because the source is often unknown, and no one offers the information.
- The isolation that brings on other mental health problems such as depression, suicidal ideations, or nervous breakdowns.
- Feeling trapped no matter the effort to move on.
- Overdosing on adrenalin and having a marked oxytocin and serotonin deficiency.
- Anxiety and toxic fear.
- Paranoid thinking and loss of trust.
- Loss of love and the right to live in peace.
- Severe adrenal fatigue.
- Overwhelm.
- Poisonous energy received by others' scorn, hatred and indifference.
- Feeling worthless, empty, and hopeless.

Everyone lives in a house of glass. Don't let the drapes fool ya. You are not alone.

* * *

3. SOCIAL OSTRACISM

If human beings are hard-wired for connection,
then ostracism is by far the most heartless of
crimes.

Social ostracism is used as punishment, when it is, in fact, among the worst of crimes. Shunning and causing apartheid is a progressive form of playground bullying. We are social beings, and often, people get ostracized without having committed a crime, or hurt the group they are shunned by.

IT IS USUALLY a byproduct of prejudice and envy. The aftermath of ostracism is denying someone the right to earn a living. The impact it has on someone's life to be shunned is slow murder. Societies that struggle with self-forgiveness and self-empathy have a tendency to shun others for the same behaviors they engage in, but haven't accepted. It is sad when someone is embraced by a foreign country that demonstrates more humanity than their own ever did.

LUCKILY, the shunned and the ostracized often flourish in their new environment. They do away with all the useless darkness they tried to reason with before. Life is too beautiful, and the world is spacious. Time is too precious to waste on things, places and people that only dim your light.

You deprive yourself of the goodness of those you choose

to banish. There are too many buried gems
among us.

4. GHOSTING

Ghosts are cowards starved for power.

Ghosting has gained popularity over the past decade or so. It is a common toxic practice, and it is to intentionally ignore someone, making them feel as though they do not exist or are not worth so much as your acknowledgment. No one likes to be on the receiving end of it, yet many practice it.

This is not the same as being distracted or not responding to every little text or call. Ghosting is methodical and a planned disappearance of someone often preceded by a promise or a seemingly positive exchange between both parties. The one who ghosts does not offer a warning, an explanation and is usually not bothered about the confusion they will leave you with. They are essentially thinking solely on avoidance and their inability to simply tell you the truth. Some think ghosting to be less painful than to outright reject someone, but what part of leaving somebody in the dark sounds better than knowing what to expect?

They have to deal with the pain of rejection and the pain of being discarded. Ghosts waste your time as you wait, find excuses, and hold on to your faith in them. Being discarded in this brutal manner leads them to question the validity of all the time, emotions, thoughts and energy they spent with the ghost. Although this method has been mainly used in the dating and social scenes by immature, spineless individuals, it is now common practice in the professional world.

Someone may take an initiative and call you about a job opportunity you have been praying for, only to later learn that they have no intention of following through. Ghosts toy with people's emotions and energy without regard, and often, with no remorse. It is especially hurtful for those on the receiving end, causing feelings of ostracism and rejection. However, it has a negative impact on the perpetrator, because they burn bridges, as well as deny themselves access to a potentially valuable and honest individual.

Mental health professionals consider ghosting to be a passive-aggressive form of emotional abuse, a type of silent treatment or stonewalling behavior, and emotional cruelty.

So if you are on the receiving end of ghosting, know that it says nothing about you, but about the ghost. At the first sign of ghosting, cut the ghost off right away to avoid further abuse. Set your boundaries straight. They did you a favor.

* * *

5. Gossiping

> Much of our problems would disappear, if we began
> talking to each other, instead of about each other.

Whether it's mindless or intentional, all gossip is malicious. Everyone knows the difference between sharing and gossiping. The former is when we share our stories, or how we feel about something; whereas gossip is something you would never say to the person directly. It has malice of intent to ruin your image and elevate their own. The target suffers a series of psychic attacks, and feel spiritually imprisoned by others' interpretation of who they are.

Mindless gossip creates the same end result because you are impacting the way others view a third party, who is not there to defend themselves. It is a cowardly act.

The gossiper cannot evade the damage either. What you say

about yourself and others is your internal mantra. What you choose to listen to, becomes a spell cast on your mind. What are you saying?

A magic spell is called a spell because words do just that to the speaker and the listener. Speak ill and you become ill. Speak well, and watch yourself elevate into well-being. What you do not forgive in another, and what you find offensive, is pointing at something you have not healed in yourself. What are you spelling? What are you doing?

> Your opinion of me will never change the truth of
>   me, but sooner or later, it will change the
>   reality of you.

This is not to say that what you say about someone is what you are. It is simply a testament about who you are, how you think, and what you oppose. At the end of the day, all opinions are subjective. The trouble begins when we forget that and make it out to be a general fact.

> *Do not hold us both hostage to the kaleidoscope of your*
> *ideas of what we once were and still must be.*

* * *

6. BETRAYAL

> Heartbreak Syndrome is real. Betrayal is a dirty
>   murder done clean.

Betrayal of trust wears many different cloaks. The sting of betrayal is sharp because it can only come from a trusted person. Spousal cheating is shrugged off. Friends discuss with others what we shared with them in confidence. Family members bail on you when you need them most.

When we are betrayed by someone we trusted for a long time, and the shift seems sudden, we won't know what triggered it, what changed, and wonder how they dared. We question all their past intentions. We can feel self-righteous and justified when we cut them off. When the betrayal is great, we feel the pain of not being able to trust them again.

In case of spousal betrayal, we can often bite the bullet and refuse to let go of the relationship, yet unless we have the power to truly work together patiently to rebuild the trust, we will turn the relationship into a constant battlefield, with distrust and suspicion eating away at our hearts. But when we are betrayed as a result of betraying ourselves, it is even more painful. Trusting someone, before they earned it, is an act of self-betrayal.

We have to be willing to confront ourselves, before blaming someone else. We teach people how to treat us by how we treat ourselves. If you share something in confidence with a new friend, the message you are giving to them is that what you shared is not valuable enough for you to protect. Sometimes we overshare just because a new acquaintance seems friendly and understanding, and possibly because we have no one else to vent to. Anyone can be friendly in the beginning. Exposing yourself to betrayal by your own hands, is like drinking poison and hoping for the best.

We have a hard time believing people when they show us who they are. We fear truths we are not ready for. If people are inherently selfish, and have a history of self-deception, then trust cannot be freely given. Once betrayed, we need to tread carefully, but not necessarily covertly. Open, uncomfortable, conversations about how we feel is better and less uncomfortable than silence and secrecy. Things do dissipate when exposed to the light.

Betrayal is often obscure. It is not always about backbiting. It can be losing trust in someone to hold space for you when you need it. We need to trust that others will not dismiss us when we need to be heard, and trusting they will not shame us for trusting them in the first place. What's more important than that is trusting oneself, and keeping the faith that no matter how many betray us, we will be ok as long as we do not betray ourselves.

* * *

7. PUBLIC HUMILIATION/GROUP BULLYING

Human degradation was at the heart of every war
rooted in discrimination, hatred, and tyranny.

Social media created a fully equipped platform for public humiliation. I am not blaming technology, but how some people showed us humanity's most malicious ways. It is one thing to humiliate yourself and to pay for your mistake; however, when people use social media to bully, humiliate, slander, and threaten complete strangers is a true virus of the heart. Maybe a good portion of humanity has always been this malicious, and our innocence was only taken away by witnessing that on a daily basis. Sometimes, I would watch a useful educational video, and notice people commenting negative and nasty things about what the speaker looks like, is wearing, or something completely irrelevant like that. The direct offender is a lot less dangerous than those masked attackers having no other focus but to take you down.

Even if a person had committed a crime, I believe those, who stampede on them are more callous than the defendants themselves. It's certainly understandable if you lost a loved one to murder, or have been assaulted or raped, to rage against the offender. But this is a different mindset than to feel glee at the downfall of another. Public humiliation and bullying are, once again, among the gravest of crimes against humanity. It is delusional and arrogant to grant ourselves the right to demean each other.

* * *

8. Victim/Survivor Shaming

Are you spiritually cross-eyed? Because your
finger is pointing in the wrong direction.

We may not be able to reason with a rapist; they got prison for that. However, we can reason with a society, hell-bent on victim shaming. We must keep on raising awareness, to hold space for victims, and help turn them into empowered survivors. It is the victim that needs to be empowered, yet we continue to embolden predators. We can no longer put up with a mentality that shames survivors back into victimhood. Sexual education must be taught at some point in schools and in the home.

Open conversations can be the best prevention. It can no longer be stuck in a loop of shame to such a degree that we subject our children to further abuse. When we don't discuss this topic, while neglecting to instill a solid sense of worthiness in children of both genders, we might just as well openly advocate for rapists and victimhood. Worthiness is a crucial foundation for sexual health. Without a sense of self-worth, people wouldn't assault, rape, or engage in voyeurism. Guilt and shame do not belong to the victim; although they are often assigned to them. These emotions are the root cause why many victims don't come forward, and are at the root of predatory behaviour just the same. If we stop using guilt and shame altogether, and replace them with just repercussions, we may have a chance at a healthier existence.

9. MURDER BY SUICIDE

To her, summer was the coldest season.

Suicide is often motivated by the desperate need to end emotional pain. Suicide is plaguing more and more of us now. I remember a time when I used to talk about suicide, and rarely did I meet someone, who felt the same. Today, I receive a concerning amount of emails and calls from friends and strangers, who are reaching the end of their rope.

All the aforementioned forms of abuse can easily push someone over the edge. We look to each other for support, but emotional invalidation is a frequent reply. We can no longer take on added pressure, not realizing that pressure mounts from lack of communication, not by sharing it. When we are another dismissive agent to our loved ones, and accuse them of being dramatic and overly sensitive, we are teaching them not to come to us anymore for guidance. What happens then is that they will pretend to be cheerful and well whenever they communicate with us. So often, we are shocked by someone close suddenly taking their own life. "But he/she seemed so happy!" This is what we often say, and now we know why. This is not to guilt anyone about it, but a clarification is needed for prevention.

There are many amazing people out there, who have a severe aversion to uncomfortable conversation. No one is expected to offer something beyond their capacity; however, they are expected to, at least, refrain from making it worse. Most friends would understand when you are unable to receive them at this time. Pay attention to whatever is most urgent, still.

I didn't want to die, sir. I just didn't want to exist
here. Just let me find my way home.

* * *

10. CRIMES AGAINST THE SELF

When our need for connection overpowers our
sense of worth, we keep destroying ourselves,
and hope to get saved.

Self-harm, suicide attempts, procrastination, perfectionism,
addiction, and people-pleasing, are all crimes directed at
oneself. Promiscuity is higher up on that list. This applies to
both genders. A lack of self-worth is often at the core of these
issues. We are taught to value others more than we do ourselves,
and put others' needs above our own. We are conditioned to
sacrifice our emotions in the name of peace. Women are raised
to be people-pleasers, and discouraged from rocking the boat.

WE KNOW who we are through the relationships we come to
know, and should they be unhealthy, so will our self-image be.
Looking for the next one to love us is our way of uncovering
parts of ourselves that our current and past lovers haven't. Your
current partner once reflected back the beauty they saw in you,
and when their vision doesn't reach all of you, you go looking
for fresh eyes to validate you. Every person we meet will tell us
nice stories about who they think we are. We take the
juxtaposition of everything we have been told and piece the
puzzle together. But if we feel elevated by other people's words,
we allow ourselves to be debased by them just the same.

· · ·

JUST AS MUCH as we are what we eat, we are who we sleep with. In the age of information on spiritual education, it is time to protect our children from themselves and others, without shame and blame. Raising insecure children make them vulnerable to emotional predators. Love fraud and cons of the heart are praised as men, while vilified in women. Women and men alike are ridiculed for falling for a player, which pushes them into shame and further heartbreak. Sex is a purging agent that brings out what's inside much like alcohol. This is why some cry, laugh, become sadistic or masochistic. It is their chosen method of release as opposed to going to the gym. Exercise purges thoughts. Sexual activity purges emotions.

TO BE with a good partner is crucial to emotional and energetic health. A bad partner who projects and enables your shadow is toxic. This is why a love fraud is often described as intoxicating. Both emotional energies merge into a mess of abusive relationships and human to human addiction. It is never too late to course-correct. Just the way food detox cleanses your system and energy, so will sexual detoxing. Some things eat away at our soul, sex and alcohol being two of the worst. When we explain to our children why valuing themselves is important, and clarify the repercussions of being emotionally reckless, they will be more likely to value and protect themselves. Shaming only prevents education and understanding.

BEWARE THE ABUSER, who penetrates your being without physically touching you. They reel you in by seduction and then denial. You get hooked on the idea of them, and they dangle the carrot of intimacy until you fall into a trap. Seduction of the mind has driven many to the brink of insanity. We owe it to ourselves, and our bodies, to preserve it as sacred land, because, we deserve better than that. Refusing to educate your children on this sensitive topic, and imposing the threats of shame, only contributes to the problem. Some manipulative people have mastered the skill of manipulating their energy. They know how to send powerful vibes toward their target, which causes the target to make the first move without knowing why. When asked, victims have reported being in a magnetic daze, and the energy was too powerful to resist despite the absence of any other positive qualities or pleasant physical features in the manipulator.

> Whenever you find yourself idealizing another,
> walk the other way before you abandon
> yourself.

* * *

EMOTIONAL ABUSE

> Who said those, who do you harm, or think you
> harm, sleep well at night? Darling, they don't
> sleep. They pass out.
> And in their comatose state, they build homes for
> cancers waiting to confront them at an
> optimum time for redemption.
> Just be sure never to harbor neither joy nor pity.
> They, of all people, deserve your forgiveness,
> but not your attention.

All abuse is emotional abuse. Whether it's verbal, physical, sexual, mental, financial, or spiritual, our emotions take a serious hit. It usually goes unnoticed. It is a favorite method among narcissists because there is little to no evidence pointing against them. In fact, it points to the victim as they are methodically driven to psychotic breaks. It is hard to comprehend why we still have to explain the complexity of abusive relationships to those, who judge the victim for it. There are so many factors involved that is near impossible to just leave. No one enjoys being abused. There is what is familiar and what is unfamiliar, and the distance to healing can be filled with traps, detours, and learning curves. You can help them cover half this distance by refraining from making it tougher on them to come forward.

* * *

The Abuse Ruse

> The man reeks of mental illness. I can taste his
> pathology... Goes well with my palate.

It is gradual and it is skillful. When the victim finds the courage to escape, the world often echoes back what the predator was saying all along; "the world is cold, judgmental and dangerous; no one will love and protect you like I do."

An abuser doesn't look or act like one early in the relationship. He appears as a knight in shining armor, who makes her feel special by sharing his vulnerabilities. Female abusers masquerade themselves as helpless princesses, who will trap a man, only to deplete him of his life force and everything he owns, including himself. Oxytocin, the love and trust hormone, is released. This natural chemical is the reason for the intensity of her emotions for him, and the illusion of trust she gets trapped by. He plays her mind against her on a chemical, molecular level, which turns her into his addict. No one understands what is happening to her, and neither does she. But the way the world responds to her only intensifies her addiction to her abuser because others make her feel judged, belittled and alone. He becomes her only refuge, and this is how he reels her in.

> *Where do you run to, when your only savior is your*
> *very perpetrator?*

PSYCHOPATHIC, NARCISSISTIC, AND SOCIOPATHIC ABUSE:

- Charm: turns into intimidation
- Interest: turns into manipulation
- Love Bombing: turns into isolation
- Protectiveness: turns into control
- Compliments: turns into verbal abuse
- Passion: turns into rage
- Vulnerability: turns into neglect
- Idealization: turns into devaluation/defamation
- Friends: turn into Flying Monkeys

MANUFACTURED INTENSITY

They create intensity by making everything urgent and rushed. They rush to get physical, move the relationship faster; get married, sharing your bank account, getting your passwords, and urge you to tell them everything about you and your family. You think it's intense and intimate, but it's not. What they are really doing is confusing and grooming you to later use you up and destroy you.

MODUS OPERANDI OF A LOVE FRAUD:
- **LOVE BOMBING**

> If you think it's too good to be true, investigate it
> and you will know. Slow down. Observe. Wait
> for evidence.

In the beginning, narcissists will crash into your life, shower you with attention, compliments, gifts and promise to make all your dreams come true. He wants to put your relationship in high gear, claiming you are the one. Love bombing is used by bosses, who are looking to exploit their employees, and by a new acquaintance, who level jumps the friendship to gain favors. They may be a flying monkey of the narcissist, who help spy on you.

• GASLIGHTING

> *Once they push you into insanity, your life becomes fair*
> *game.*

This is methodical and pre-meditated crazy-making behavior. As depicted in the film, "Gaslight" a narcissist would dim a gaslight gradually then light it up again. When his wife would ask why the light dimmed, he would tell her she is imagining things. They make you question what you see and hear.

THEY HAVE no problem denying doing what they are doing right before your eyes, and their audacious denial makes you question your sanity. You lose trust in your senses, because he is your only link to reality. Gaslighting occurs after you are successfully isolated from your support network. He tells you what is real and what is not. The more you think you're insane, the more of a recluse you become, and the more vulnerable you are to further gaslighting. You don't find anyone else to affirm you. This is done gradually with little things and before you know it, you are completely insane. He can now control and get away with everything with ease, and not worry about you witnessing any of it.

• ISOLATION AND EXCLUSION

> Show me the distance between your wound and
>   your skin.

This happens early in the relationship. First, the love-bombing will keep you busy, as you spend most of your time together in a honeymoon phase. As you spend less and less time with friends and he consumes more and more of your time and attention, your friends and family may feel left out. When they complain or get bitter, you will make the mistake of sharing your stress with your new lover. This is the opportunity he has been waiting for, to demonize those closest to you and justify isolating you from your support network. He won't say it directly, of course. He may defend them and tell you to be more patient with them. He is a talented predator. Later down the line, he will hint how they must be jealous of you, and make you reach false conclusions about your loved ones. He will drain you and upset you, so they, too, decide to stay away from you. When they do, you start to think he was right about them. Once you are isolated, because your friends don't know how to be around you anymore, he will then exclude you from his own activities. He can finally keep you isolated without having to be physically present.

• REACTIVE ABUSE: DOG WHISTLING

> It is the most sneaky of crimes when all evidence
>   points to the victim as the prime suspect due to
>   their reaction to the pain they were subjected
>   to.

Dog whistling is when the narcissist says something covertly hurtful that only you understand to make you appear crazy, oversensitive, sad for no apparent reason, and people find you depressing. They use this tactic especially when you are having a good time, being the life of the party, and laughing from your heart. Narcissists do not like it when you laugh, and certainly don't want you to impress anyone with your intelligence, wit, and humor. They will instigate a fight, sometimes, before going out, as a pre-emptive strike. Dog whistling is used to get you to react. They may invite you out just to bully you. They make you appear as the abusive one, so that people believe the lies he will tell about you later. People may wonder what you do behind closed doors if this is how you behave in public. Lacking insight, your social circle is drafted to be his soldiers. They are the blind sighted flying monkeys. Dog whistling doesn't have to be something whispered. A narcissist can take jabs at you in front of others. But they do so in a seemingly light-hearted manner, making you the butt of their jokes. When you do get upset, you will be accused of being overly sensitive. They didn't mean it that way, they say. Can't you take a joke?

• TRIANGULATION

> *They will flaunt their new supply, and idealize*
>   *everyone else but you, because it is you they want to*
>   *keep.*

Anyone, who dated a narcissist, will know all about

triangulations. They compare you to others in a negative way, making you feel less than, and that you will never be as beautiful, intelligent, or worthy of love as their ex or new love interest. They flaunt their new love in front of you to further break you. Other narcissists in your life such as friends or family members use triangulations differently. They pit people against each other, and single you out as the odd one. You are excluded from gatherings, and deliberately not informed about important developments that concern you. In a job environment, your boss brings in someone barely qualified to gradually take your place. The new person is introduced as your new assistant, but shortly after, you are not invited into meetings relevant to your project. If you confront a narcissist about triangulations, they will either deny it altogether, or accuse you of being aggressive, even if you're not. Next thing you know, you are completely cut off.

As PAINFUL AS it can be, don't engage in such infantile behaviors. Cut your losses and move on. The narcissist cannot care about anyone, including the new supply. Time will expose them without your effort to get justice.

• STONEWALLING AND SILENT TREATMENTS

Stonewalling, and the silent treatment are favorite methods of the narcissist to bring you down to your knees, begging for them to acknowledge your existence. Ghosting is when they disappear on you. Stonewalling is when you are in the same room, but they act as though you don't exist. You try to talk to them, but they manage to look right through you. At times, they give you the dead stare to intimidate you before you say what you want to say. It can be something as simple as asking them how something works, or if they want to eat. Stonewalling is an abuse tactic that is often unprovoked. It's only to keep you on your toes. The narcissist is easily insulted. If you outshine them in some way, or disagreed about something frivolous such as not liking the same food they like, they decide to punish you. Stonewalling, done publicly, they exclude you from a conversation. They joke, and flirt with, and compliment everyone else, but you. They do not address you at all. If you join in the laughter or conversation, they make sure not to laugh, often frown whenever you speak, and when you finally notice, you go silent to figure out what's going on.

The silent treatment is not always silent. It is giving you short and sporadic answers, claiming things are ok when they are clearly not, and not involving you or initiating any conversation with you. All of the above are passive-aggressive methods. It's a psychological sleight of hand if you will.

• PASSIVE-AGGRESSION

> If someone is too spineless to say no to your face,
> they cannot be trusted with anything else in
> your life.

This includes agreeing to help you when they have no intention to. They waste your time knowingly and then play dumb, claim they forgot, or pretend to be angry or busy so you don't ask them for anything, not even an explanation. It can manifest itself as deliberate poor performance so that you have to redo the entire task and not bother asking them for their input in the future. It can range from washing the dishes, helping you meet a deadline, or picking up the kids from school.

IN FACT, they may find ways to distract you to deliberately

sabotage what you need to accomplish. They talk to everyone about you, but not to you, and talks to you about everyone else. They create rifts between people, so that they can control everyone in their circle, and become the one everyone else confides in.

• DEVALUATION

Your value is by what you have to offer and what
no one can take away from you.

When you know your inherent value, no one else can devalue you. Those, who devalue you, are showing you what they lack within themselves. This is what abusers do. When you remove yourself from the equation and listen to what they're saying as confessions about themselves, it will be the most honest account you can receive, if you are willing to receive it. Do so with grace.

WHEN YOU TRULY VALUE WHO you are, you will not feel the need to throw their insecurities in their face, nor will you accept their devaluation. When someone offers you a pill filled with poison, you do not have to take it off their hands and swallow it. This is their story. You are not asked to make it your own.

THE LACK of self-love and sense of self-worth are at the core of every poor decision we make. It is by far the most important sense we need to develop early. Children know their worth by how you treat them, and not what you say to them. Show your love, respect, and appreciation, even through challenging times. It can save their life.

When someone wants to bring you down, it means they perceive you as above them. They want to take away the things they see in you that you have not yet seen yourself.

• INTERMITTENT REINFORCEMENT: BENCHING

Inconsistency creates addiction.

In and out, hot and cold, something is not working right with that faucet. Scarcity breeds addiction, and they use it to get attention. Unhealthy people know that should they be available, their mask will slip. It rests heavily on their face, and they need to put it down away from you. Someone made them believe their real face is unlovable. So, they refined themselves a mask. They put you on the bench to guarantee they won't lose you. Should they get comfortable enough to show you who they are, they will show you what they believe about themselves, often in the worst of ways. The moment they know for certain that you can see through them, is the moment their abuse will escalate and the roller-coaster of the love-bombing highs and the devaluation lows will be more nauseating than they ever were. When someone is playing games, don't play. When they can't decide what they want, make the decision for them, and leave. This ride can only end in sickness at best. Listen to the early red flags, and if you do see one, and dismiss it, ask yourself why it wasn't red enough for you.

One person's red flag is another person's comfort zone.

• DISCARDING

A narcissist never discards you, unless you want to see it that way. Whether you are aware of it or not, you always initiate the discard by ceasing to give them supply or you no longer fall for their bullshit. There is nothing to be proud of being the primary narcissistic supply. Ask yourself what you think you deserve, and if this is not it, then ask why you are sacrificing this much for something that is not for you.

• WITHHOLDING AFFECTION

Narcissists use affection as a means to an end, and the end is always control. Somatic Narcissists are preoccupied with physical contact as their main source of supply. It makes them feel desired. Withholding affection is a way to make you feel undesirable. It's used as punishment. They may spend months not so much as holding your hand. They sit at a distance, and act disgusted if you try to hug them, or pat them on the back when they act upset. They treat you as though you are a contagious disease; a hobo, or a rabid dog. They resent you for offering any form of intimacy, no matter how innocent.

But if you reject them, they become aggressive. They rape their spouses to let them know they cannot be rejected and often do so to humiliate and inflict pain. Spousal rape is the worst of its kind because no one wants to acknowledge it. They ignore your boundaries, blackmail you, and find ways to prove they own you. They often threaten to cheat, and flaunt new partners in front of you just to torture you. It makes them feel valuable and powerful.

Never offer a narcissist intimacy. It is grounds for punishment too. Since they want to uphold the illusion of superiority, you risk shattering that by daring to act as their equal, and worthy of their intimacy. Anyone showcasing abusive behavior only gets worse with time. Cut your losses sooner rather than later. It is not your job to walk on eggshells, or preserve their massive and fragile egos.

• HOOVERING

Narcissists love to come back. They think life is a revolving door with an open buffet made just for them to indulge in. When they return, it means they miss your supply, and your particular recipe. It may mean they are running low on supply in general. The main reason they disappear in the first place is not necessarily that they met someone else. It might, but sometimes they disappear around the time you saw through them, or tried to call them out on their behavior, or caught them red-handed in a lie. They must disappear so you can't hold them accountable. Depending on the nature of the incident, they will calculate how long they need to disappear for before you stop caring about the issue. They tend to have a heightened sense for your desperation. When your need for them to return to you overpowers your need to blame them for their abuse, they reappear.

At the beginning of a relationship, they do the disappearing act as a scarcity tactic. By the time they reappear, you're just glad they're here, which makes you more likely to adhere to their timetable, and oblige their immediate requests. We all know that new person, who makes plans, but rarely follows through. They send a minimal text, with the least amount of effort, and expect you to be at their beck and call. The scarcity tactic is passing on their urgency to you. "I'll be traveling tomorrow for a couple of weeks, so let's meet tonight!" They may or may not be traveling, but if they are, you can be sure you won't hear from them when they return, unless they can get away with stringing you along in a casual relationship. Don't take the bait. You can waste the best years of your life with someone offering you nothing but crumbs. The methods they use to hoover, vary. The overt type will make grand gestures, tell you all you want to hear, do all the things you asked for before, and may even propose. (Please say no.)

If they are covert, they may use a third party to get to you in a staged coincidence. They may have a flying monkey casually tell you that narcissist is sick, or had an accident, so you break no contact first. The covert type does not do anything directly. They are not nearly as audacious as the overt type, but a lot more sneaky. Some people feel rejected when the narcissist does not "hoover"; however, it only means the jig is up, and you finally began to recognize your self-worth. It is a positive sign when a narcissist wouldn't dare return to abuse you again.

• SPIRITUAL/PSYCHIC ATTACKS

When all else fails, just poison them with doubt.

Draining someone of their life force, using religion and spirituality to control and ridicule are ancient effective tactics. When people respond to you from a religious point of view, it makes you reluctant to respond. In fear of being shamed, and accused of lack of faith, people drop the debate. Using black magic, or hinting that they would, is enough to make you sick. It's a scare tactic that works. Their energy is powerful, and they know that all they need to do is instill doubt.

* * *

DISMISSING DEMEANING WORDS SUCH AS "DEVALUATION," "hoovering," and "discarding" is a good start to respect yourself.

You are not an object to be evaluated, a doormat to be hoovered, or trash to be discarded.

No Contact

The most effective solutions for saving yourself from these human snakes and hyenas is to go completely No Contact, and to clean up your wounds. If there is an original narcissist in your life, like a parent, you need to tend to the wound they left you with so you don't continue to attract narcissists and sociopaths. If not, then look at whatever is not healed within you.

If you raise your vibration, you will not be necessarily vulnerable to predators. Still, some of the healthiest people can fall victim to those without conscience, because they see the best in everyone. They believe people are inherently good, and are unable to comprehend the depth of human evil. Take your time, and let people show you who they truly are, and be sure to believe them.

Self-protection is paramount. Abusive partners and friends are branches that will naturally fall away when you get to the root of the tree that is making you sick.

No contact is not the same as silent treatments. It is self-preservation, that is not done with the intention to hurt the other person. It is to protect yourself from an abuser, who refuses to resolve issues or be accountable for anything. How many failed attempts at reconciling will it take for you to realize you are dealing with a child of Satan? Every person has their own timeline, and I hope you reach the conclusion before more damage is done. Remove yourself from toxic situations, and protect your privacy at all cost. You do not need them for closure. This is how you tap into your power, by stripping them of the power to put your mind and heart at ease. You do not need it. I promise you this much.

*What lies beneath your shadow that's giving birth to
    your fears?*

* * *

NARCISSISTIC VICTIM DISORDER

I thought the world of you... A world of pain.

Anyone can be victimized by a narcissist or a sociopath.
Often, intelligent, successful, joyful, and empathetic people are
walking targets. Predators are attracted to and challenged by
light. Here are some criteria that manifest in a healthy person
after being subjected to narcissistic abuse:

- You don't recognize yourself.
- You are depleted.
- Brain fog.
- Constant rumination.
- Feeling it's your fault.
- Chronic stress.
- Depression.
- Feeling empty.
- Low self-esteem.
- Addiction due to intermittent reinforcement.
- Shame passed on to you from the abuser.
- Nightmares.
- Dissociation (as a coping mechanism).
- Easily triggered (trauma response).
- You develop addictions to numb.
- Self-destructive behaviors.
- Fear responses. Panic attacks.
- Seeking validation due to a lack of self-trust.

I wasn't sure if I wanted to love him or kill him. I had a sword and a pen. I went with the sharpest.

THE HUMAN MAGNET SYNDROME

An abused person internalizes their abuser, which may cause them to become magnets to other abusers.

Narcissists choose people, who are more likely to fall in love with those, who hurt them. It is human nature to seek validation from those, who don't like us, and please those, who refuse to respect us. This is rooted in our primal need for connection. In the beginning of time, connection meant survival. This is just as true today; however, we forget that our network is wider, and that we don't have to rely on the unreliable. We have access to each other more than ever, and we do have options. Emotionally scarred people, who have not been taught to value themselves early on, grow up believing that love is pain and punishment, and that they have to settle for less.

> "Children are like dogs; you knock them around enough, they think they did something to deserve it." ~Sawyer, LOST/J.J. Abrams

STOCKHOLM SYNDROME: LOVING THE ABUSER

"Was he the love of your life?"
"No, he's just another one of my sins."

Defending an abuser has puzzled law enforcement and psychologists for a long time, and finally, the reasons behind it, are coming into public awareness. It's still not fully grasped;

however, especially to our social network, who were fortunate enough not to go through this complex experience. There is an element to abusers that is beyond description.

No matter how much you read about it, you simply have to be in it to understand. Anyone can be prone to abuse, and you'd be surprised at the powerhouses that were reduced to shells of who they once were.

When we are subjected to crime, the first thing we try to do is fetch for the captor's humanity. We have a firm belief that it must be in there somewhere. Many criminals love to talk because much of the criminal mind was birthed by being abused, unseen, and unheard. They have to hide behind the power of a weapon to be acknowledged. Without it, they know they will be insignificant. Ignoring your children can push them to seek significance, and they will get it by any means necessary. The violence can be directed at others or the self.

When captors tell their stories, we experience a deep sense of relief that their humanity has been retrieved. We find our own pain in their stories because we can all relate to feeling insignificant and unworthy. The bond is created by the truths within their story. When they speak of the harshness of the world, we empathize with them. We find justifications for their behavior; although nothing justifies crime. We are put at ease when we find a logical reasoning to a criminal act. A bad situation is made worse when we witness a senseless crime. Some criminals do so out of pleasure rather than pain. We cannot negotiate with those, who have no particular reason to assault and kill.

When we manage to escape, we are often subjected to the harshness of the world they were talking about. Our friends accuse us of masochism, stupidity, and point out the flaws within us that led us to attract this kind of event into our lives. We find ourselves alone, and missing the understanding and kindness the captor offered us. We were sheltered. When we have a pre-existing fear of abandonment and rejection, we find comfort by the way the captor holds on to us; and because they are truly flawed, we think we can, for once, feel better about ourselves. The methodical grooming and brainwashing of the captor creates an invisible leash. We are too terrified to rebel. This is why people return to their abusers after they successfully escaped and ended things for a while. One call is all it takes for the victim to run back. It's not masochism. It's called Stockholm Syndrome.

HERE ARE some things people say to victims and survivors that push them back into the arms of their abusers:

- You must have enjoyed it.
- How come you were able to go to school/work/the store, and still be captive?
- You like being hit.
- You just love abusers.
- You don't have any self-worth.
- You are lying.
- How could you allow this?
- My god, you are so weak.
- I can't believe you are that stupid and naive.
- Why didn't you just leave the first time?
- Maybe he was your boyfriend and you made him do this. You can be difficult.
- You have a wild imagination.
- You're the crazy one.
- I'm sure it wasn't that bad.
- Get over it already.
- You are obsessed! Why are we still talking about that?

Human psychology is a deep, prehensile labyrinth.

I advise against thinking this could never
happen to you, because, everyone else thought
the same before it happened to them.

THE ENABLERS

It takes a master enabler to become a sensational
victim.

Enablers of abuse are abusers by proxy. They can be a
codependent partner, flying monkeys, and morally corrupt
friends. When we tolerate negative behavior, we enable it.
Becoming people's crutches, we harm them just the same. Being
silent about injustice is injustice. If it wasn't for enablers,
abusers wouldn't have the audacity to cause harm.

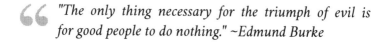 *"The only thing necessary for the triumph of evil is
for good people to do nothing." ~Edmund Burke*

CODEPENDENCY: SELF-LOVE DEFICIT DISORDER

You hurt me. I hope this muted your pain for a
little while.

You confuse your codependency with empathy. You think
self-sacrifice is love, and think his intensity is proof you found
your Twin Flame or Soul Mate. At the beginning of a
psychopathic relationship, you immediately feel ready to settle
down with this person, because you both seem to share the
exact same hopes and dreams. He sizes you up real fast and
echoes back to you everything you are. You strike an unspoken
deal: He lets you take care of him, and you never ask for
reciprocity.

But once you are hooked to this human heroin,
their mask begins to slip; and because you can't
let go of the fairytale, you will keep trying to
glue his mask back on together.

He feasts on your fears and delusions. When he finally depletes you, he will leave you. You love him because he reminded you of someone that was important to you. You love him because you don't love yourself. When he is in prison, and you marry him, knowing where he is at all times, and that he can't cheat, you feel comforted. But prison doesn't stop him, because there is an abundance of codependent princesses out there just like you and me. Maybe his toxic love is what you think is all you can get, and what you think you deserve. He can be magnetic, and a lot of fun, but his shortcomings make you feel secure that you are better than him, and therefore, he would never leave you. You're wrong. It is usually those you lower your standards for are the ones who don't value you. This is what you have shown them. Maybe you fear rejection, and maybe you fear commitment; this is why you choose the impossible so that it's never your fault when it doesn't work out. Maybe you think no one will stay anyway, so you might as well settle for scraps. You will discover, you have been wrong about everything, about him, and about yourself.

It was the psychopath in me that saved the
borderline in her.

Some people destroy you by way of destroying themselves. They destroy you as a byproduct of what they do to themselves. Self-harm has collateral damage. The question is, why are you harming yourself? What is it that is making you addicted to sacrificing yourself? Often, when we are committed to being heroes, it is to avoid taking responsibility for our lives. We secretly wish to be saved, so we save others. Codependents are self-proclaimed empaths, but are, in truth, covert narcissists, who pride themselves in Jesus-like martyrdom. They will often complain about all the sacrifices they made for others without receiving gratitude. They take it upon themselves to mother and father their partners and friends.

They think, without them, no one will make it. They have to micromanage everything. It is the ultimate form of hidden control.

Heroism is deceptive because it is never authentic. We mask our selfishness and hide it under the cloak of a superhero. If in childhood, we had a narcissistic parent, we have been conditioned that we will only be valued and accepted when we sacrifice our own needs for someone else's. We had to please the parent, or we would be banished. Codependency is a way of making ourselves continuously useful to earn our place in someone's life; often, this someone is equally toxic.

> That magical night, on our first date, he grabbed
> me by the neck, pushed me violently against
> the wall, and, nicely, invited me to sit. He took
> out his gun and pointed it at my head. 'I need
> you to listen to me' he said. He was so
> articulate, he could cross-examine a tree for
> three days. That was the moment I fell in love.
> We still have a good laugh about it.

There is nothing noble about people-pleasing when you abandon or betray yourself. Codependency is inverted narcissism. *It is an act of self-destruction to be this dangerous to oneself.*

> For addicts like these, the darkness remains
> trapped under their scars.

Self-sacrifice breeds resentment when we don't receive gratitude for it. This is because your way of giving is tainted. While others may accept whatever favors you are offering, they will not accept being indebted to you for it. The second you deny them a request, they will vanish.

It was never anything but a transaction. There is no reason to keep you when the deal is off. A healthy, authentic person will instinctively decline such offering. Those, who accept, are opportunists, and they are rarely grateful anyway. If you are codependent, figure out when you learned this behavior, and shift your focus back onto yourself. Only then, will you be able to authentically give, and repel the users and abusers from populating your circle.

OUT OF THE F.O.G.: LEAVING THE NARCISSIST:

What broke our relationship you ask? Well, I
finally snapped in his hands.

It takes an average of 7-10 trials for someone to leave their abuser for good. That's how powerful a trauma bond is.

HOW TO LEAVE:

- Use his disappearing acts as windows of opportunity to heal yourself, raise your self-confidence, and find a trusted professional to talk to.
- Revisit your own history and figure out why this relationship is familiar to you.
- See your partner the way they truly are without idealization or devaluation.
- Attribute their characteristics to someone you don't

care for, and ask if you would still find them appealing.

- Addiction is quite strong, but do whatever it takes not to pick up that phone.
- Not to be confused with power struggles.
- See that this person knows exactly what they are doing and that they do see your worth. It is your turn to see it too.
- Stay away from any judgmental friends. They will only make you more addicted to him. They are a lot worse than the abuser.
- Do things for yourself. Find your purpose, feed your talents, connect with good people, and rediscover the joy that has been muted.
- Stay away from drugs and alcohol. They compromise your good judgment.
- Do not date anyone else before you have healed.
- Don't judge yourself if you relapse. Do not beg, plead or expect anything from the abuser. Let them do what they do, and see the game for what it is.
- Remain grounded.
- Connect with other survivors.
- Talk to yourself as though you are talking to someone you love.
- One trustworthy person is more than enough.
- Ask them not to allow you to engage in circular thinking, and to be your accountability buddy.

ABUSE IMMUNITY

No one is guaranteed immunity to abuse, but there are steps that can help you better prevent it:

- Set healthy boundaries.
- Clean up all of your wounds.

- Have a solid vision for your future and hold it.
- Clearly write down what you want. Do not settle for anything less.
- Work towards becoming the person, who would attract the things you are asking for.

CHAPTER 7
SELF DISCOVERY

We know ourselves through our relationships.
Our relationship health is dependent on the
one we have with ourselves.

Relationships magnify our existing emotions. Every relationship unveils a new aspect of who we are. It is the ultimate mirror. The most important journey for us is the one within. This is why many struggle to maintain relationships. Unless both partners are committed to their respective growth, and continue to align with each other, they will succumb to betrayals to themselves and each other. I believe relationships to be the best indicator of our health, and a catalyst to the overall quality of our lives. It deserves special examination that I am reserving for a future book. For now, we take a look at the most important relationship we will ever have, and that is, with ourselves. Once we remedy that, all others will fall into place.

We can only understand and know someone as
deeply as we know ourselves.

We are all capable of everything; only everyone has a threshold to get there. But knowing who we choose to be helps us know which part of ourselves we want to feed. How well do you know yourself? There are 50 basic questions that most people should be able to answer. People are complex and filled with contradictions. However, some of the biggest mistakes we make are: 1. We assume others will be like us, and refuse to comprehend our differences. 2. Not all contradictions are possible. For example, you cannot expect a psychopath, someone who is born without the ability to develop a conscience, to show remorse. You can; however, expect a kind person to do an unkind thing.

A SUCCESSFUL CHARACTER portrayal has to be relatable, and therefore, believable. We need to be able to relate to others, regardless how different we are. We may not be able to relate to a serial killer, but we can relate to his/her fears, addictions, and vulnerabilities. The same can be applied to superheroes, whose motivations and sacrifices can be compared to our own, even if on a smaller scale. Superman can fly whenever he wants, but we relate to his sacrifice for love and his need to do good.

When we meet ourselves deeply in all its dimensions with acceptance and compassion, we will be able to offer acceptance and compassion to our loved ones. The best gift to offer your loved ones is the healthiest version of yourself. To achieve that, we must cleanse every area of our lives of toxins, be it addictions, bad company, laziness, and everything else in between. The people we surround ourselves with eventually impact us in some way, and should we choose poorly, it ends up draining our lives and dreams. Be your own best friend first, and from there, choose the best people, who deserve the best of you.

· · ·

ASKING the right questions propels spirit to offer us an answer; the more intelligent the question, the more useful the reply.

Ask yourself the following questions. Ask your loved ones the same questions and offer them your presence and attention.

I hope they unlock the mysteries you seek to know.

WHO ARE you at the core?

Is there anything you do that does not honor who you truly are?

What do you want?

Why do you want this? Why now?

When are you? (The times we live in impact us)

Where are you now? Where have you come from? Where would you like to be?

What will happen if you don't reach your goals?

What is the intention behind your goals?

What must you overcome?

How will you get what you want? (How we achieve something will come naturally, once we know what we want and why we want that. So, don't waste too much time on the "how", unless you are looking in retrospect to better understand your character or someone else's.)

50 BASIC COMPOUNDED QUESTIONS

Answer these questions and get to know yourself

1. What is your birth name? Nickname? How did you get it? Preferred name? Why did you choose it?

2. What is your birthdate and location?

3. What do you like and dislike about people?

4. Which part of you is heroic and which is wicked? Which part is usually prevalent?

5. What is your comfort food?

6. How do you dress most of the time/"dress up"?

7. What do you fear the most? What emotional scars do you have? Do you show them or hide them?

8. In your opinion what is your most redeeming feature? Meaning, what is the good quality that makes up for your bad?

9. What is your most prized mundane possession? Why is it valued? A prized possession can be anything of sentimental value, but is not necessarily valuable to others. Maybe someone you love gave you a pen or a stone, or maybe you carry a penny for good luck.

10. What one word best describes you?

11. Where do you live? Where did you grow up? What was the condition of your upbringing?

12. Who was your father, and what was he like? Was he available, alive, departed, strict, or kind? Did he provide or neglect his children? What was he like as a husband?

13. Who was your mother, and what was she like? Was she available, alive, departed, strict, or nurturing? Is she motherly or selfish? What was she like as a wife?

14. What was your parents' relationship like? Are they married or divorced?

15. Do you have siblings? What are their names? What order do you come in? Do you like or dislike them? Why?

16. What is the worst thing your siblings did to you? What was the worst thing you did to them?

17. How do you view your family? Do you feel supported or abandoned?

18. Are you close to other extended family members? Who are they? What do you think of them?

19. What is your first good memory? What is your first bad memory?

20. What was your favorite toy or past-time?

21. Are you extroverted or introverted or an ambivert?

22. Is there any non-family adult that was influential in your upbringing? Who were they, and why do they stand out?

23. Who was your best friend growing up?

24. Did you have pets growing up? What kind? What were their names?

25. What is your worst childhood memory? Were you abused in any way? By whom? How did you respond to it? Did you tell anyone? Is it still affecting you, if so, how?

26. How do you feel about authority figures? Are you compliant, respectful, or rebellious and defiant?

27. Who was your idol growing up? What characteristics do you admire about them?

28. Do you have a job? What is it? Do you love what you do? If you don't have a job, how are you financially supported?

29. Who are your closest friends? What are they like? Do you feel fulfilled by them or drained? Are they genuine?

30. How is your relationship with money? Do you save it or spend it? How do you feel about earning it?

31. What annoys or irritates you? What are your emotional buttons and triggers?

32. What would be the perfect gift for you?

33. Do you wear any jewelry, make-up, accessories, or wigs? Do you have hair, and how do you style it?

34. What embarrasses you? Why? What triggers your shame?

35. What does an ideal day look like for you?

36. How far would you go to achieve your goals? What are your goals? Are you comfortable asking for help?

37. What is your ultimate motivation? What fuels it?

38. What do you dislike about yourself? Is there something in your past you are most ashamed of? How did it impact your present and your self-image?

39. What are you most proud of about yourself? What is your biggest accomplishment? What characteristic do you have or lessons learned that is making you proud of who you have become?

40. Are you a leader , follower, or a lone wolf? Why? What is your philosophy about your preference?

41. What is the thing that makes you most anxious? Do you express your anxiety to someone, or do you suppress it? Who do you trust with it, if anyone? Why?

42. How do you feel about death? Is there anything you can think of that is worse than that? Do you love or hate life?

43. Has anyone close to you died? What happened? How do you grieve? How do you celebrate their memory?

44. Are you quiet or outspoken? Are you private or do you overshare? Why?

45. What is your greatest weakness? What makes you break your boundaries? Is there someone specific you tend to break your boundaries for? Why?

46. Do you have any bad habits, addictions, or reckless behaviors? What are you addicted to? Why?

47. What would you do if you won the lottery? Are you currently wealthy, poor, or average?

48. Do you believe in fate and destiny? Are you religious, spiritual, or antagonistic?

49. What are your short-term goals? What are your long-term goals?

50. Are you the best version of yourself? If not, what would you be like? What do you think is missing?

BEYOND THE BASICS

1. If you have one speech to tell the world before you die, what will you talk about and why is this so important for you? If you free write about your emotions, what comes out?

2. What are the concepts you feel the most passionate about? Is it justice, kindness, courage, etc.?

3. How do you view time? Can you be present in the moment or do you have difficulty staying grounded? Why?

. . .

4. WHAT IS friendship to you? What would you never tolerate in a friendship?

5. When you pray, who do you pray to and what for?

6. What is love to you?

7. How do you interpret God? Male, female, or transcending gender? Is it synonymous to Nature or Consciousness, or something separate? Why? Are those your ideas or were they embedded in childhood?

8. Since we can die at any given moment, how would you like to spend your final moment on earth? How would you like to be remembered? Who would you want to spend your final moments with? What would you say? What would be the most significant thing?

9. Are you sensitive to energies? What is your energy like? What raises it and what debases it? Would you be eager to better yourself or heal, or are you numbing with drugs, or going through the motions on survival mode?

10. Have you been diagnosed with any mental, or physical illness? Do you have a personality disorder? How do you deal with setbacks? What speech would you give about an inspirational journey you went through or if you have defied the odds in your life?

11. Is your country the best fit for you? Why and why not? Do you feel home? Where do you feel home? Which country is a better fit for you?

12. What would people say about you in your funeral? Is it something you would be happy with?

13. How do you feel about animals? Do you fear them or love them? Can you communicate with them? Are you connected to Nature?

14. What secret do you want to take to your grave? Why? What would happen if it becomes known?

15. What is standing in your way to reach your highest potential or your fulfillment? Are you a grateful person or a complainer? Do you blame others for your misfortune or do you have self-responsibility?

16. How can you empower yourself? What are you doing now or saying that is disempowering you?

17. Is there anything you do that harms others? Do you project your pain onto the world? Do you put other people down, or do you have integrity and purpose?

18. What have you not forgiven? How do you define forgiveness? Is there something you cannot forgive yourself for? What do you want others to forgive you for?

19. What is your home emotion? What is the root cause of it?

20. Who do you truly want to become? What are you willing to sacrifice or let go of for your best life?

REMEMBER, *when you ask any question in life, you have to be still to hear life's reply. Sometimes, we get stuck in a loop of questions, and forget to stop and listen. Other times, we ask a question, but then get distracted when we are being answered. Try it for yourself with a friend, and if you have children, you will understand even more:*

Let's say, someone asks you "Are you going to the party?", and then kept asking the same question in a loop. I want you to keep trying to answer the question, but you keep getting interrupted. Your friend doesn't stop to hear the answer to their question, or maybe they ask once, but when you answer, they walk off into another room.

THE UNIVERSE OPERATES MUCH *the same way. It is always replying to all of our questions. We just have to be quiet, and truly listen. Once you ask for something, make sure you are meeting all of the criteria and energetic frequency that aligns with what you ask for.*

Everyone wants to find Mr./Mrs. Right, but how
many are willing to be the right one?

BOUNDARIES

Boundaries are the glue that keeps all virtues
intact.

It takes an average of 40 years to learn healthy boundaries, and a few more to apply them with consistency. The quality of your upbringing plays a major role in how long it takes to create a set of healthy boundaries. Most of us have not been taught healthy boundaries, because our parents' generation was still getting the hang of it, and that's the best-case scenario. The worst-case scenario is being raised in an environment with unhealthy or non-existent boundaries.

FOR US TO ACQUIRE VIRTUES SUCH as courage, empathy, integrity, and authenticity, we have to create a set of boundaries that are healthy. Unhealthy boundaries are not adhesive, which will not maintain said virtues. Knowing your boundaries and values will help you navigate through life easier. It is important to keep going back to your list to make sure you are applying them. As you grow and gain more life experience, you may need to update your list. Life lessons come in spirals, meaning, with every stage, we learn deeper truths about the same lesson. It is an endless process. Keep a boundary journal as your guide. Remember to enforce your boundaries on yourself, not just on others. For example, if you have a boundary to commit to your work, you must decline an invitation that may distract you. Do not expect others to refrain from overstepping your boundaries. They can only do so when you allow it. Every boundary you create, you have to determine a consequence for breaking it, whether by you or another.

Boundary Examples

Keep the entrance door guarded, and the exit door open.

Emotional Boundaries

1. My emotional well-being is a priority.

2. No tolerance for any form of abuse in my relationships. I guard the gates to my life, and those who enter are free to go.

3. I take responsibility for my emotions, and will not look for someone to make me happy.

4. I do not dismiss my emotions when they arise. I will tend to them with kindness.

5. I will not allow my negative emotions to overstay their welcome.

Spiritual Boundaries

1. My time for solitude and reflection is sacred.

2. I commit to Meditation, and will not allow anyone to interrupt me.

3. I will not allow others to intimidate me into their beliefs or energetic vibrations.

Physical Boundaries

1. I must take care of my physical health.

2. I listen to my body and honor it.

3. I do not tolerate anyone invading my physical space.

4. I will not allow anyone to shame me for my body. I will love it and respect it. I owe it to no one else.

5. My home is my sacred space. Only trusted people allowed.

MENTAL/PSYCHOLOGICAL Boundaries

1. I will feed my mind with good things. No junk information.

2. There is no tolerance for negative self-talk or circular thinking.

3. I honor my quiet time and will have zero tolerance for noise.

4. I do not entertain people, who play mind-games of any kind.

5. No more complaining. Ask others to point it out if you start to complain rather than share.

SOCIAL BOUNDARIES

1. I expect to be treated with respect.

2. My circle is small. Trust must be earned.

3. I must treat myself and others with respect. If I fail to do so, I must make amends.

4. My social life is a place for joy and idea exchange.

5. Zero tolerance for gossip, slander, or bullying.

PROFESSIONAL BOUNDARIES

1. I expect the highest standards of myself.

2. My life's work must remain at the forefront.

3. I do not accept work I don't love.

4. I know my worth and the value I add to others. I refuse to settle for less than I deserve.

5. I do not allow others to take advantage of me.

6. I expect people to remain professional, and not drag me into personal dramas.

ENERGY & TIME

> Energy is our life force. Time wasted is wasted
> forever.

Now that you have your own list, make sure you have fitting consequences for boundary-breaking. For example, if you do not tolerate it when someone calls you names, the consequence can be cutting this person off, or limiting your interaction with them. You have to communicate your boundaries clearly and in a healthy manner. Make sure the person understands it and its consequences. None can read your mind. How you communicate your boundaries is crucial.

* * *

THERE ARE some telling signs of unhealthy boundaries:

1. If you rage against someone, who didn't know of your boundary.

2. If you give the silent treatment or use other passive-aggressive behaviors instead of talking to the person.

3. If you say yes when you want to say no. Instead, you disappear.

4. If you always try to keep the peace no matter what is going on. You can't please everyone. It can turn into resentment.

5. If you are intrusive and enmeshed with people, and ignore signals of their discomfort. When you barge into a conversation uninvited or invade someone's space.

6. If you break your own boundaries for someone you like, especially if you don't know them well enough.

7. If you ignore red flags of sneaky behavior in others and then complain when you get bitten.

8. If you procrastinate and waste others' time and your own.

9. If you make false promises and intentionally deceive others long enough to use them, or until you get out of the obligation.

YOUR BOUNDARIES ARE your sole responsibility. They are unique to you. Create your list and keep on empowering yourself.

DO NOT ALLOW anyone to drain your energy or waste your time, including yourself. It takes one area of drainage that would deplete your entire life-force, and resources. Time, can never be replenished. Depleted energy eats away at our time.

THE LIST IS endless and will vary from person to person. Creating boundaries can be fun, and is a great opportunity to be your own best friend. There is a variety of material out there to help you create your own. Make sure not to duplicate someone else's boundaries, if they do not resonate with you.

One man's deal-breaker is another man's deal-maker.

CHAPTER 8
PROCESS & INTEGRATION

INTENTION SETTING

> An intention is the decision to energetically align
> with the desired result. The accuracy of your
> alignment, determines the quality of your
> results.

There are no good and bad intentions. It is the level of internal
agreement we can reach that makes it so. It is either aligned or
misaligned. Intention is different from an objective. Whereas an
objective is about what we want, our intention may or may not
be aligned with what we want. The world of intention goes
beyond the notion of right or wrong, good or bad. We are in a
state of intention setting at all times; however, we are not
always conscious of it.

* * *

ALIGNED INTENTION

An aligned intention means your mind, body, and soul are in complete agreement on a certain action or goal. You have full presence and focus. A serial killer, who sets out to find his next victim, is fully aligned. He enters a house, commits his crime, and leaves. Mission accomplished. What he did was bad for others, but the result was in positive alignment with his objective.

MISALIGNED INTENTION

A misaligned intention is when you are divided and fragmented. Your mind, body and soul, are at odds with each other, creating cognitive dissonance. You may want one thing, but believe in its opposite. You can truly want to do something good for someone, let's say, you offer to clean their house. But because you are misaligned, possibly your mind was elsewhere, you set the house on fire. What you set out to do was good; the end result is bad; your intention was out of alignment.

NOTE: Absolve yourself from anything and anyone that doesn't honor you or your path. Then shift your focus to setting your intentions properly. If you decide to be more graceful, more successful, kinder and healthier and more loving, your behavior will shift. You will see yourself in a way that asks you to raise your standards in every area of your life.

METHODS TO UNFOLDING

- Grounding
- Meditation
- Visualization and affirmations (keep the affirmations

in the positive rather than saying what you do not want, say what you do want, in the present tense, and be mindful of what follows I AM this or that)
- Music that aligns with heart rhythms and nature's flow. (432Hz, for example, is a positive frequency among others)
- Free Writing
- Release the Screen
- Create an inspired life
- Connect with your essence, Nature, and animals.
- Energy Work (Be careful who you entrust your energy with.)
- Read the code of ethics of Native Americans
- Read Martial Arts code of ethics and Self-Mastery techniques

Remember: Healing is never linear.

Do not get discouraged when you revisit an old lesson, fall in the same trap, regress, and relapse. Life is a spiral, and it is best to approach it with humbleness, kindness, patience, and grace. When you learn a lesson, understand you learned it as deeply as you were ready to receive it, and know, there's always pending further information.

INTEGRATION

Check in with all parts of you to ensure peace agreements are in place, and lead the collaboration. Allow them to harmonize as you orchestrate a masterpiece of your life.

Prayer is when we reach out to the divine.
Meditation is when we shut up and listen.

* * *

EPILOGUE

Gratitude was the gateway to everything great.

Gratitude must show in our actions, behaviors and emotions, not just our words. It allows us to shift our focus away from scarcity, and into appreciation. Being in this state, invites more things into our lives to be grateful for. All things have valuable lessons that are essential for our involution. Looking for the lessons, we find value in our stories. Never let a great story go to waste. Much love and gratitude for sharing in this journey with me. I wish you healing.

AYAHUASCA PRAYER: CÉU DE AMSTERDAM
This is what the sons and daughters of the Earth have the right to ask for; Life. Health. Happiness. Open Paths.

Health in the Body. Peace in the Spirit. And Love in the Heart.

It is this that we wish for ourselves, for our loved ones, and for all of our brothers and sisters.

So be it. And so it is. Namaste.

ACKNOWLEDGMENTS

Produced by Marco Salem and J.S.Wolfe
Cover Design & Logo by Nadine Soliman
Published by Involution Publishing
Printed by Elias Publishing

ABOUT THE AUTHOR

J. S. Wolfe is a writer, filmmaker, and coach, with a specialty in character analysis. She is passionate about true crime, personality disorders, consciousness and shamanic medicine.

She attended UCLA film school, and worked with several esteemed artists in the film industry; Cornelia and Martin Bregman (Scarface), Vincent Vieluf (Rat Race), Khaled Elsawy (Yacoubian Building), among others.

Her articles were published in The Village Voice, The New Yorker and DAM. She wrote creative press releases for international fine artists such as Susana Rodriguez (Argentina), John Silver (NYC), and Miki (Japan) during her work at 48th Avenue Art Gallery in Manhattan thanks to curator Mr. Alejandro Beitler.

Ms. Wolfe is committed to her healing journey, in order to be of better help to others on the path. Her message is, we are never alone, if we know where to look.

facebook.com/JSWolfe.Author
twitter.com/JudittaWolf
instagram.com/involutionbooks

ALSO BY J. S. WOLFE

The Pathology of Innocence (Spring 2020)

About: Transcending the Smoke & Mirrors created by Narcissistic Abuse, the Mother Wound, and healing Relationship drama.

Dear Psychopath... (Winter 2020)

About: A crime novel, based on true crime stories, fictionalized through the imagination of a 7 year old boy, aspiring to become as significant as his idols on death row.

Made in the USA
Middletown, DE
23 October 2023

40970749R00182